SHE SITS
SHE RIDES
SHE FLIES

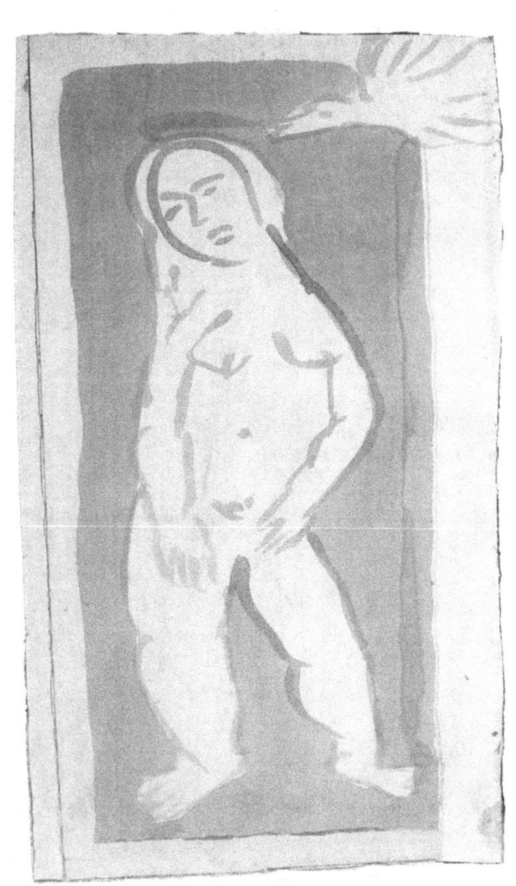

**ARTWORK
PETER SCHUMANN**

**NARRATIVE
ELKA SCHUMANN**

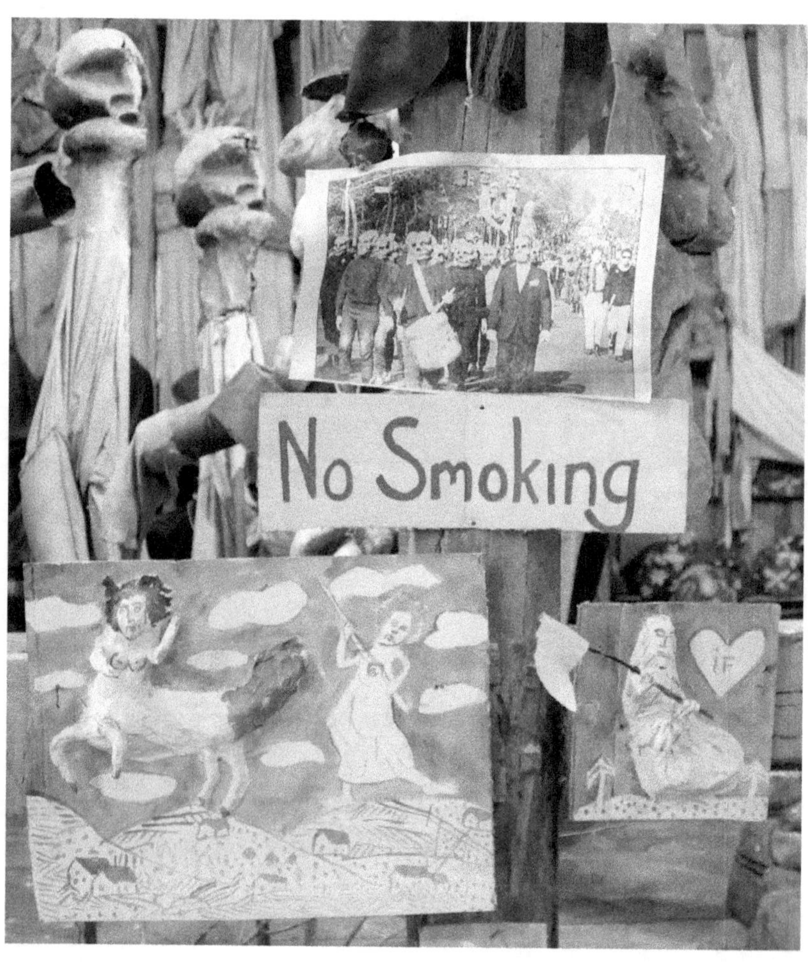

No Smoking

SHE
SITS

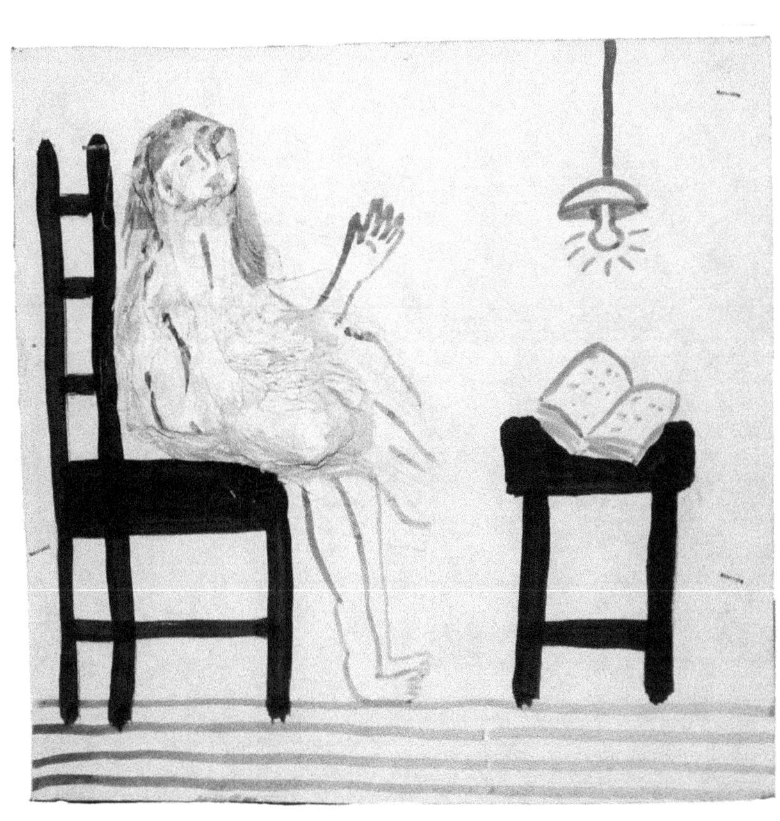

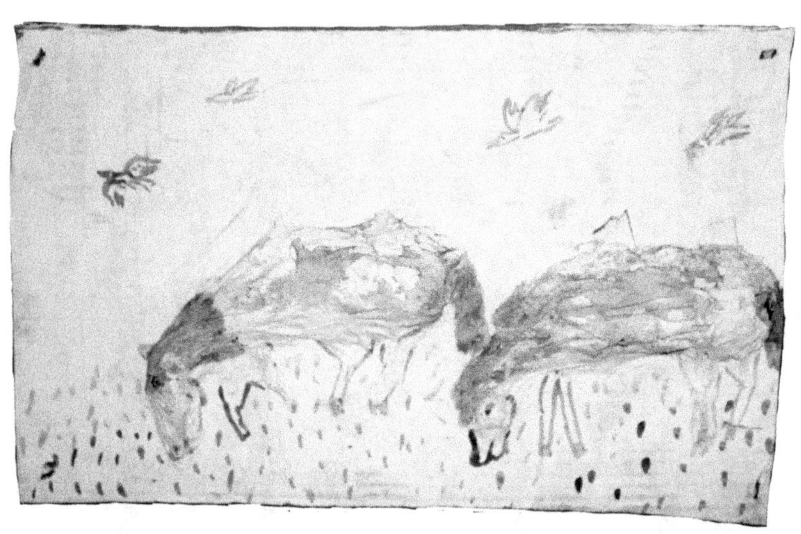

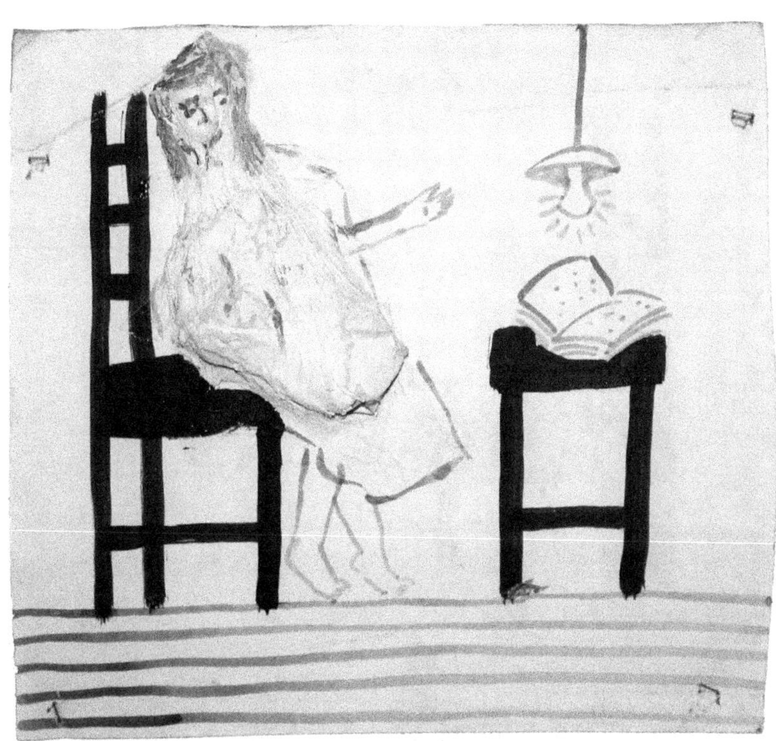

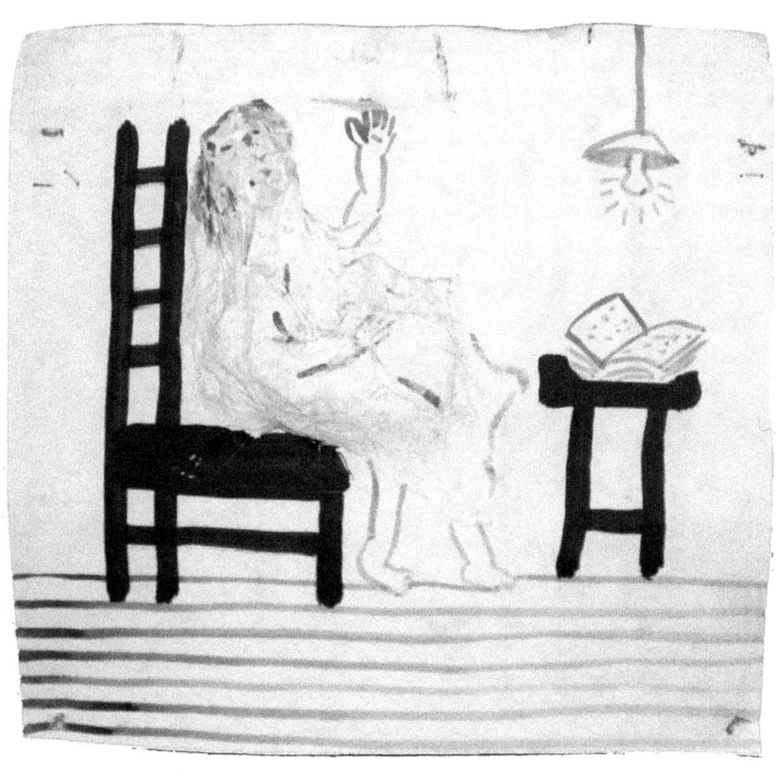

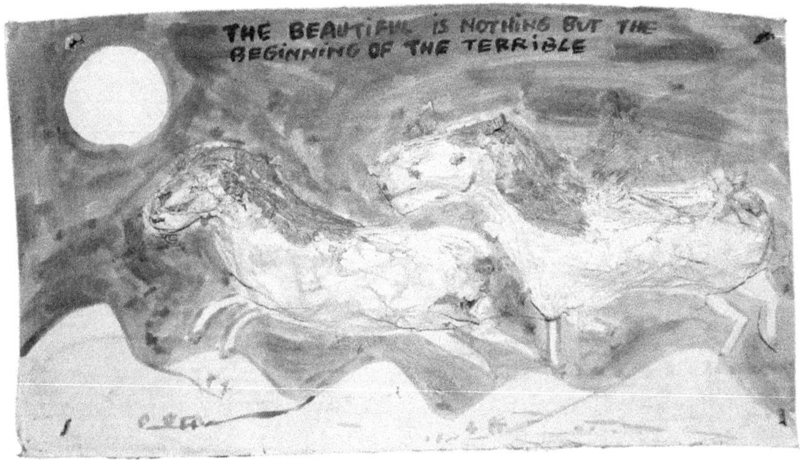

I am Elka Schumann. I was born on August 29, 1935, in the city of Magnitogorsk in the Ural Mountains. My legal name is Leigh Scott, but I've been called Elka, my parent's nickname for me, most of my life.

EARLY LIFE — My father was an American college dropout who wanted to travel to this new Communist world in the Soviet Union to help build the new society. Before he left America he took a course at General Electric in welding, so he could come with a useful skill. He traveled first to

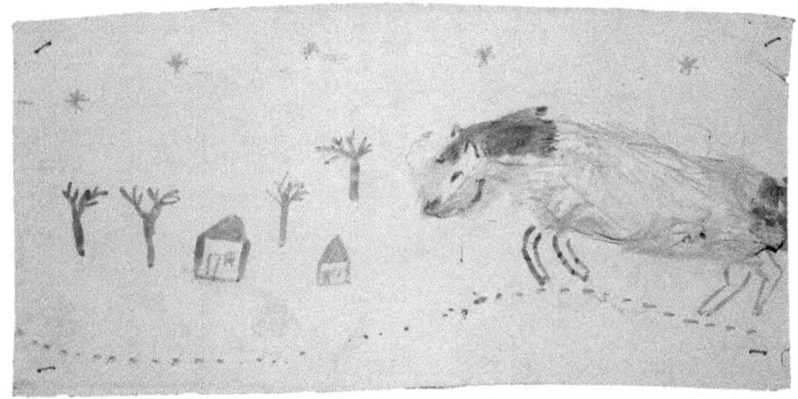

Moscow and then was sent by the Soviet state to Magnitogorsk, which was a big industrial place where they mined iron and coal and built machinery.

My mother, Maria Dikareva, was a high school math teacher in Magnitogorsk, where my father was working in a mill, and also in the office. There's a funny story of how they met. My mother would also come to this same office, sometimes to help out, as her sister was the wife of a manager of the mill. There, she saw a list of people's names who

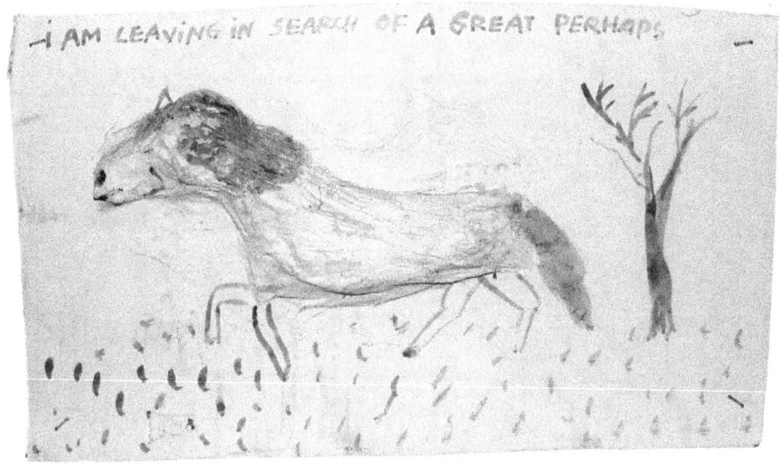

worked there, with a new name: John Scott. In Russian, Scott is Skot, the name means cattle; it's not a nice way to address anybody, but she was intrigued by it and asked a friend to point out who this was. She imagined some kind of glamorous movie star man, but instead she saw this skinny, bespectacled guy and immediately felt sorry for him, that he came from this terrible society, oppressed and exploited by the capitalist system. And that's how they met.

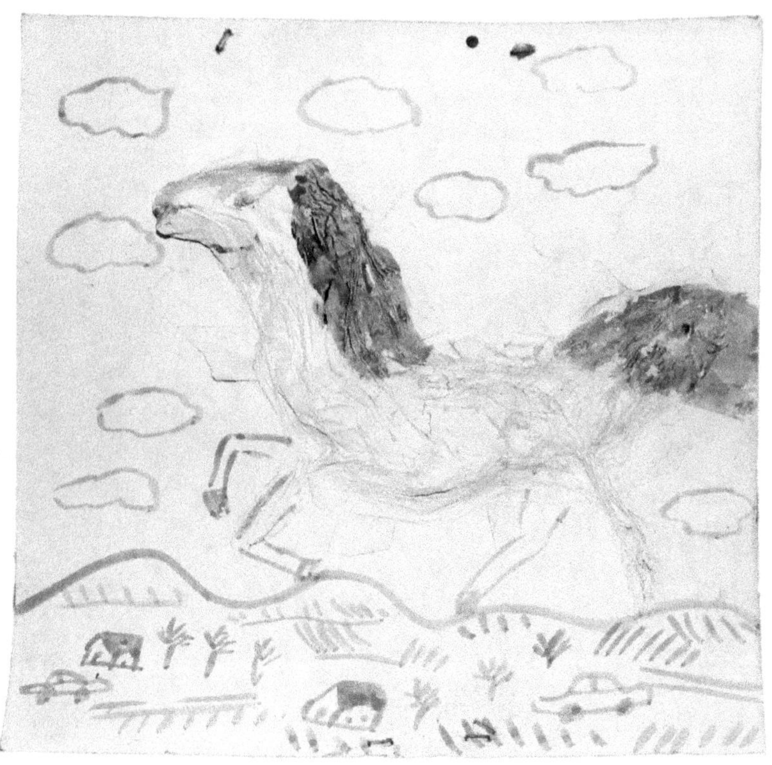

I have a very vague memory of Magnitogorsk. I remember being taken for a walk to a hill, and there was a snowstorm. But later my parents told me there weren't any snowstorms when we walked that day — it was a sandstorm. We left Magnitogorsk when I was 3, so I hardly remember anything except that glimmer of sandstorm.

My father, because of the purges, lost his job in Magnitogorsk and decided to leave the Soviet Union. My mother wanted very much to get

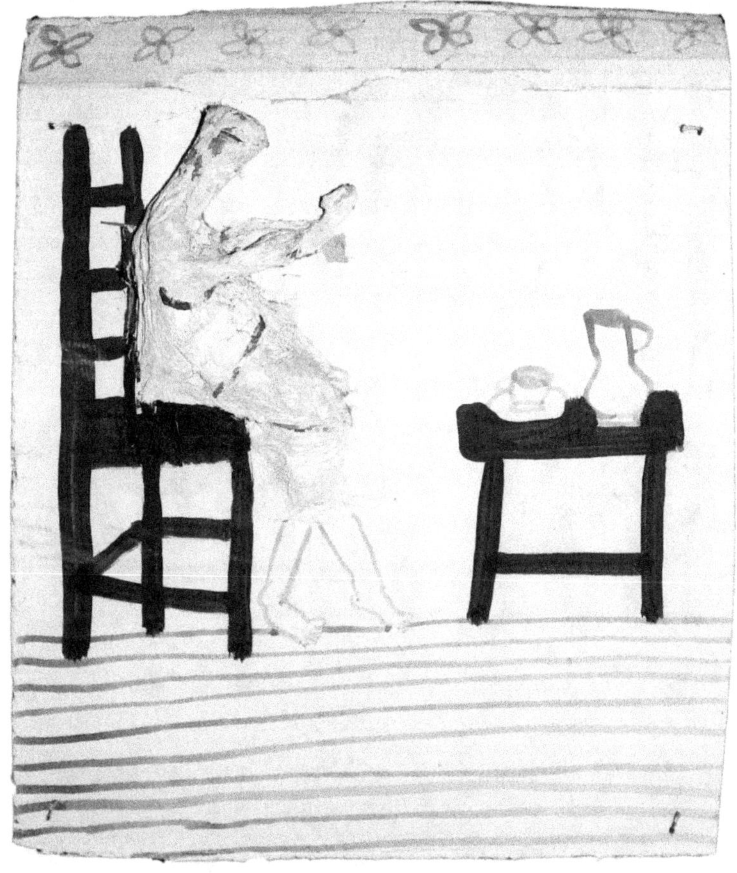

out of there as quickly as possible, because she was afraid for her safety, and her two children, my younger sister, Elena, and me. We had a 3-day train ride to her home village, Udomlya, part way between Moscow and Leningrad, where my mother had grown up, and her parents still lived. I remember some little children's songs that sound like they might have come from that era when we moved to my mother's village.

I have pretty vivid memories of my grandmother. We lived in a

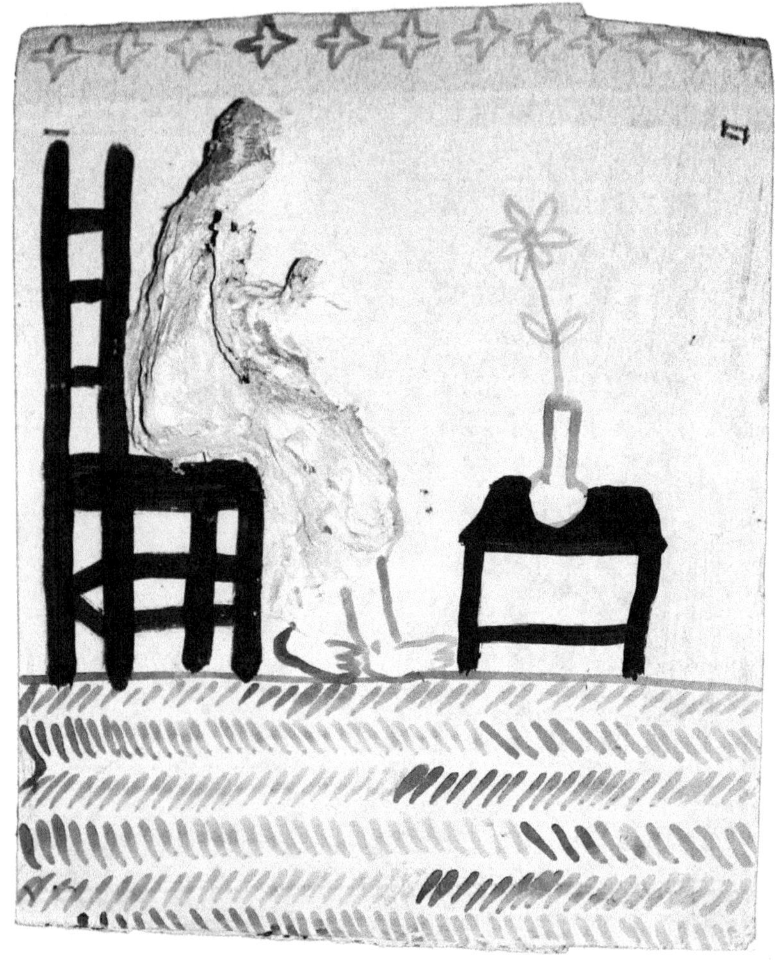

simple Russian log house with no running water. So the water was fresh from a spring that was nearby. And I didn't want to wash my face or something. And she sort of grabbed me by the scruff of my neck and hauled me over there to get me cleaned up, and I was screaming all the way.

My grandparents were peasants; their children had wonderful educational opportunities under Communism: all my mother's nine siblings

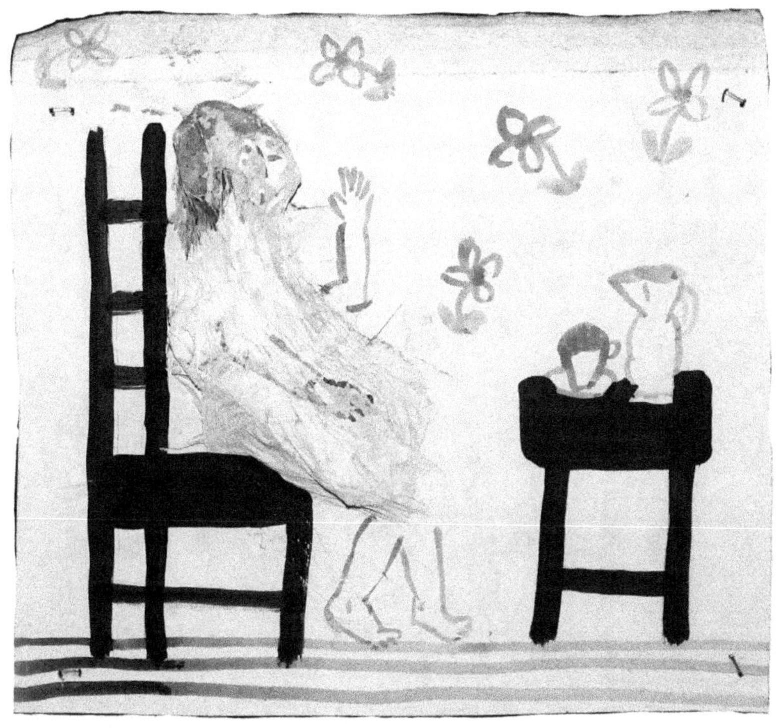

ended up being doctors, physicians, engineers, dentists, and teachers because they were able to get an education.

I remember my grandparents' village.

My Russian grandfather, Ivan Kalinich, was an illiterate peasant. His wife, my grandmother, Yekaterina Ivanovna, learned to read &write in her late 40's or 50's from her own daughter, Tanya, who was the village school teacher. Her handwriting looked like a child's writing.

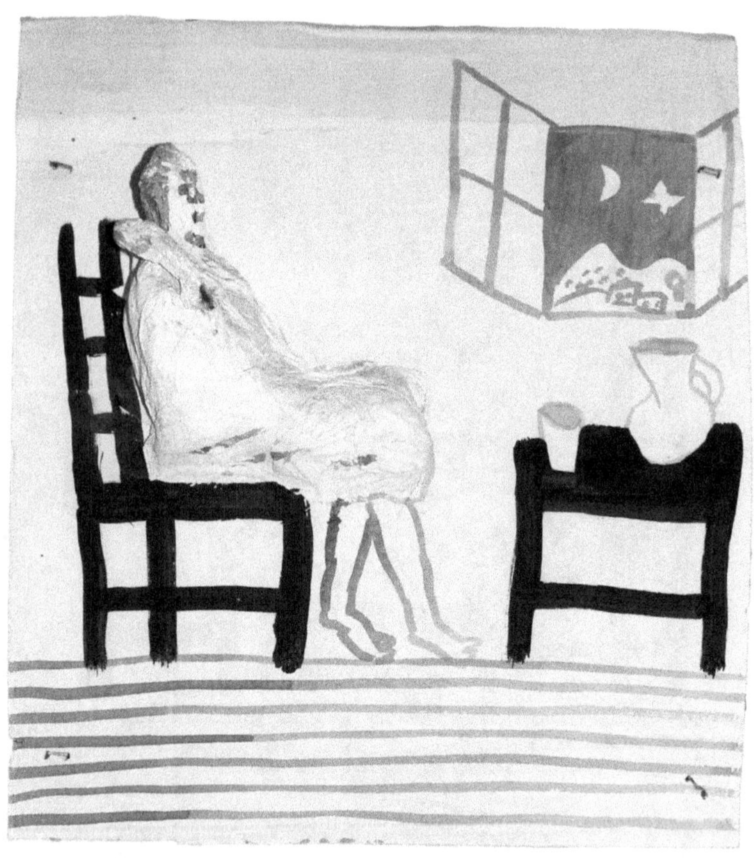

After that, we moved to Moscow and I remember going to the Kremlin. My father worked as a freelance journalist. I think of it as a glamorous life, because we went to the Kremlin for special celebrations. I remember seeing the "Nutcracker Suite" there, that was very memorable. And Christmas parties and other celebrations for my sister and me.

It was while in Moscow that my father wrote a news report on the meeting of Hitler and Stalin that led to the Hitler-Stalin Pact, which

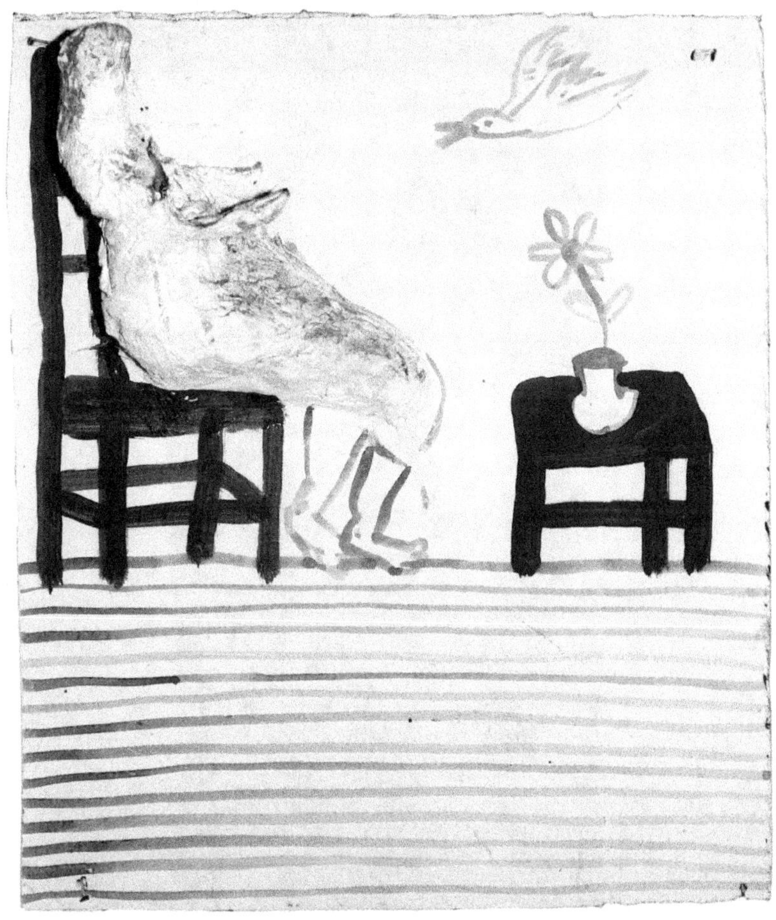

Stalin went into to avoid the war that he felt was coming. But the fact that my father wrote about it was looked on as incorrect by the government. It was breaking the censorship regulations, and he was ordered to leave the country.

My mother had been trying ever since Magnitogorsk to get a visa to leave with her two children, and finally when she got it, we all left. We took the train from Moscow to Vladivostok. It was 10 days on the train,

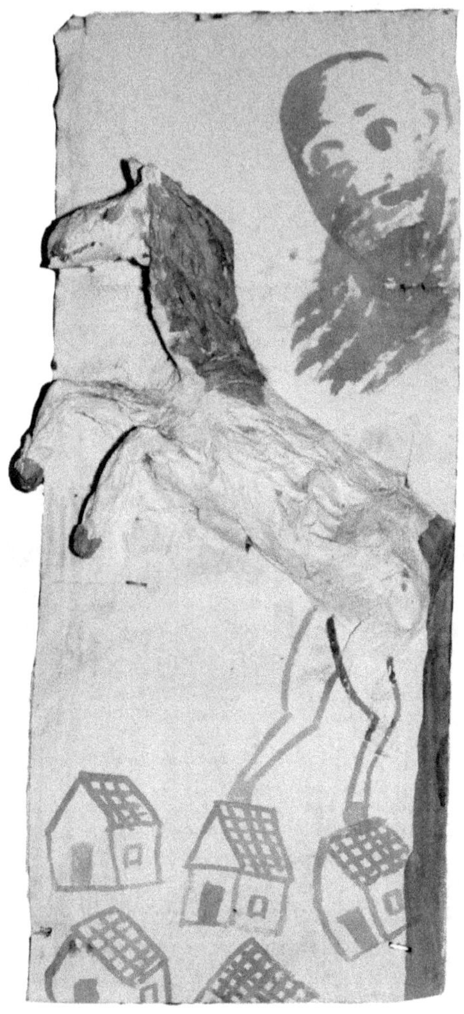

stopping in stations in little county towns along the way. The peasant women were standing by the side of the tracks bundled up in quilted jackets and all selling whatever they had to the passengers — train foods, fried fish and buns, breads and things like that. The person who shared our seats with us was a man who had an injured leg or maybe amputated leg and I remember being reprimanded to be careful of him and not try to crawl over him or whatever. But I don't have any, you know, nightmare

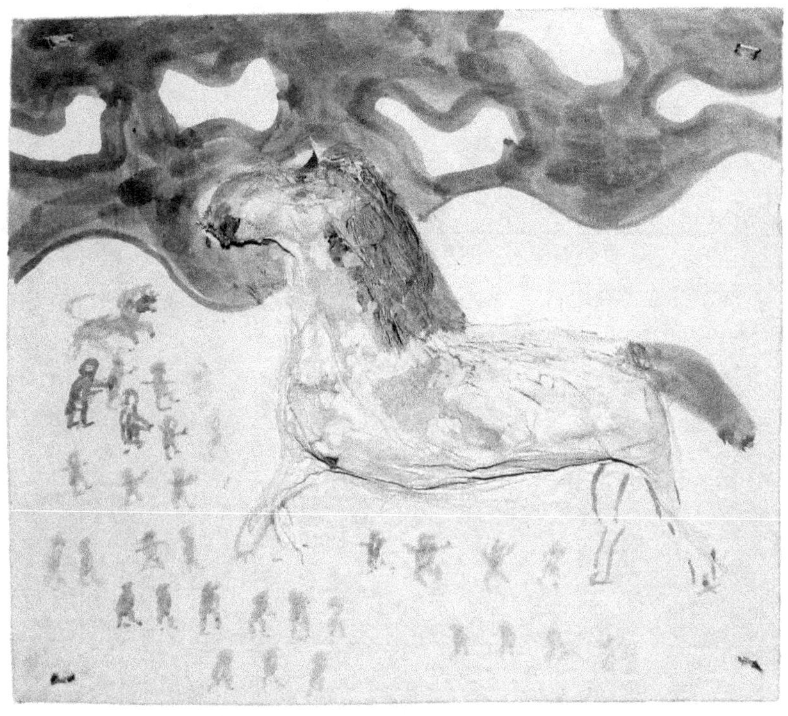

memories of that. It was exciting. Small children on a train for 10 days. That must have been quite an ordeal for my mother.

MOVE TO AMERICA — We arrived in Vladivostok and got on a Japanese ocean liner to go to Japan. It was 1941, just days before the Nazi armies attacked the Soviet Union, so if we had stayed, even for a few days, we probably would not have been able to leave. We ended up in Japan for a couple of months waiting for a boat to leave from there to go east

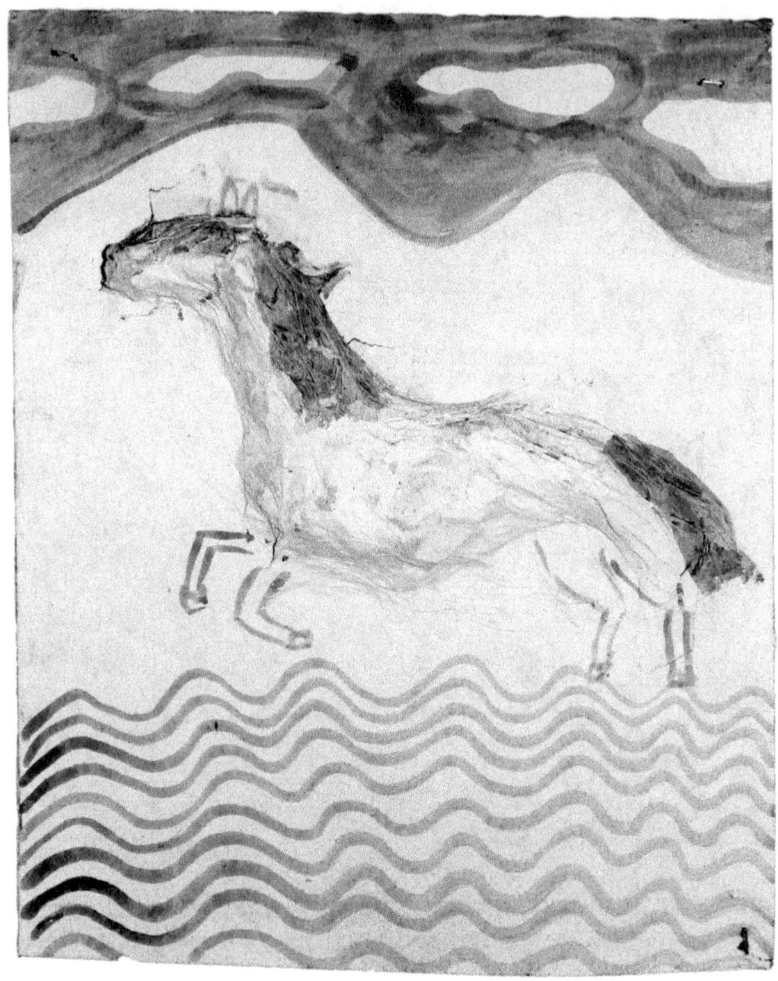

to Hawaii, and then to the United States. My sister and I got dolls before we left Moscow, a girl doll and a boy doll, and the girl doll had hair and somehow on the short boat trip from Vladivostok to Japan, the doll fell into a puddle on the deck. And sailors came and tried to scrub the doll clean. I was very upset about it. Memories come and go like that. And then in Japan, we actually stayed for quite a long time, maybe a month, waiting for a ship that would take us to the U.S. because by that time,

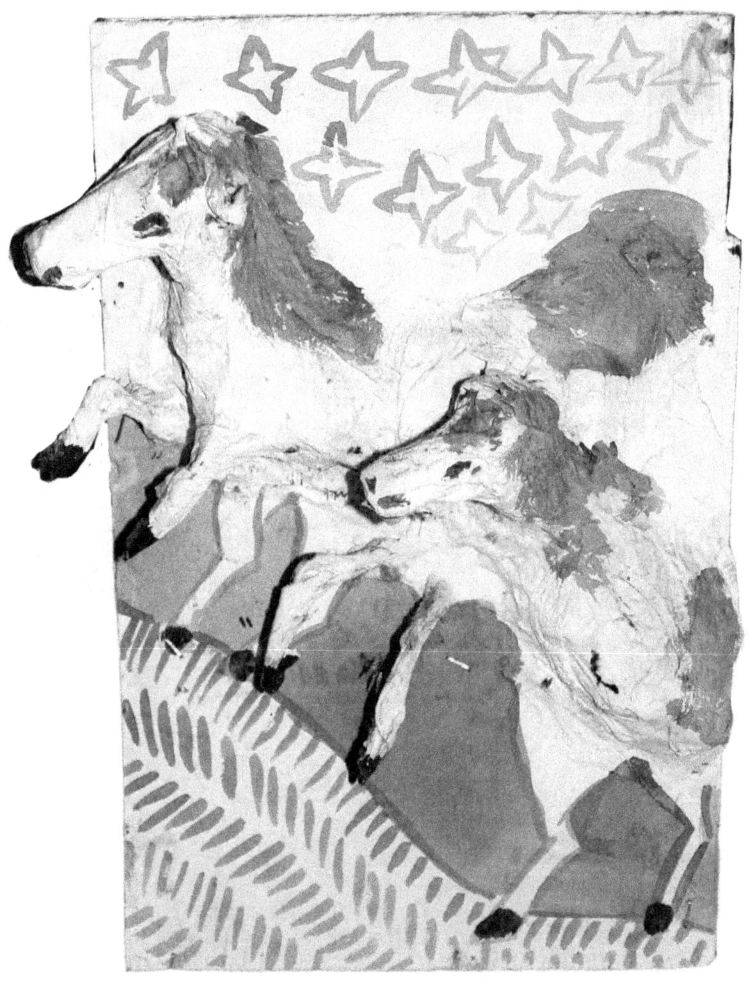

relations between the U.S. and Japan were quite tense. And then, waiting for a boat to the U.S., I remember going to a Nō play and seeing these very interesting things, and how they changed the scenery. They didn't close curtains or anything, they pulled the blue rug that was the river out from under a bridge and carried the bridge away. That's what I remember there, and being at the beach, and also the very, very strange food that was not like anything we'd had before.

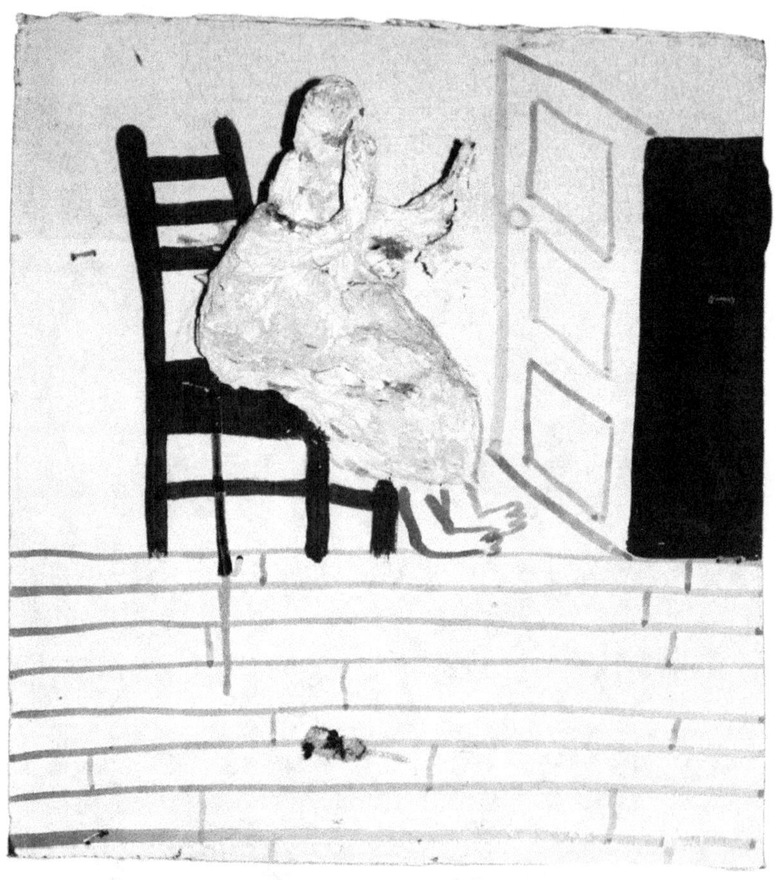

That was an adventurous journey because several times the sun was on the wrong side of the boat and I realized that the boat had turned around and was going back to Japan because of all the tension there was. And then I think a couple of days later, when I got up in the morning, the whole boat had been painted in camouflage overnight.

But we made it to Honolulu. Pearl Harbor hadn't happened yet, but things were very tense between America and Japan. All the passengers

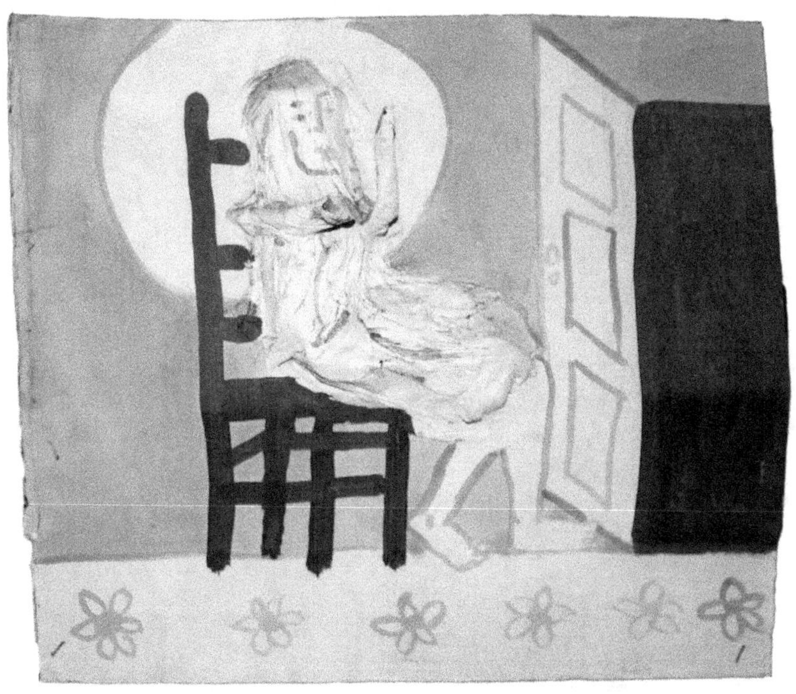

were very, very eager to get to Hawaii, for then they would be safe from the dangers of war. We arrived there and then got to San Francisco and took the train east, to where my family was.

I'd like to emphasize that my mother did not flee the Soviet Union. She was a staunch Communist. She and her whole family had benefited from Communism, with education. I remember always hearing about the vacations workers got. They'd be sent to the Black Sea resorts for weeks at

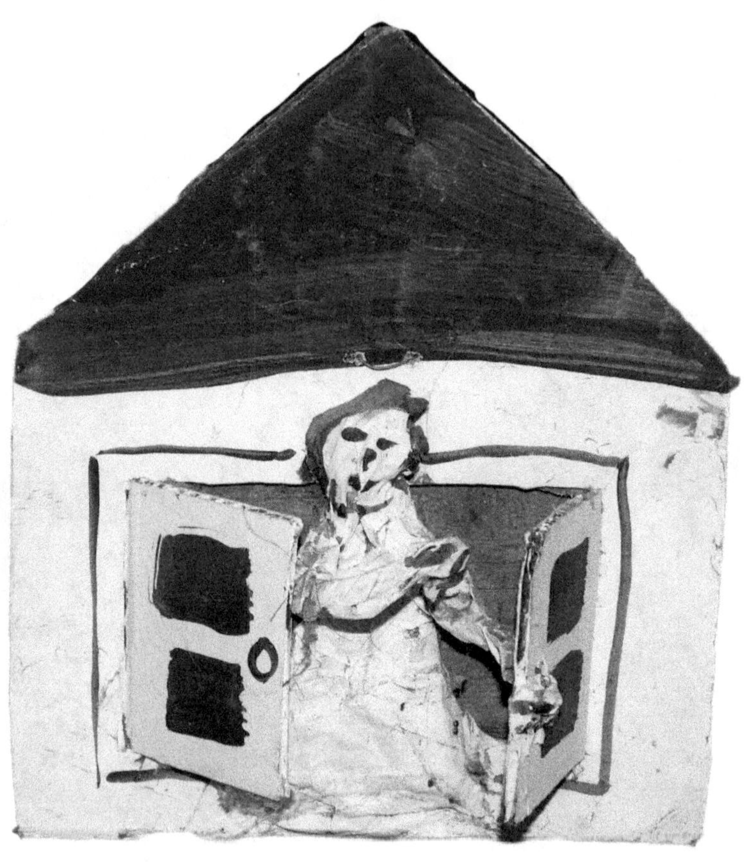

a time, with full pay. She wasn't politically involved in Communism, but she definitely benefited from it. She wasn't a refugee.

We ended up at my uncle's farm in upper New York State. My Uncle Bob, my father's brother, was a farmer and we lived in the farmhouse with my Uncle Bob and Gene and their two children. I went to a one room schoolhouse for a little while.

We stayed on there with Uncle Bob on the farm in Willoughbrook,

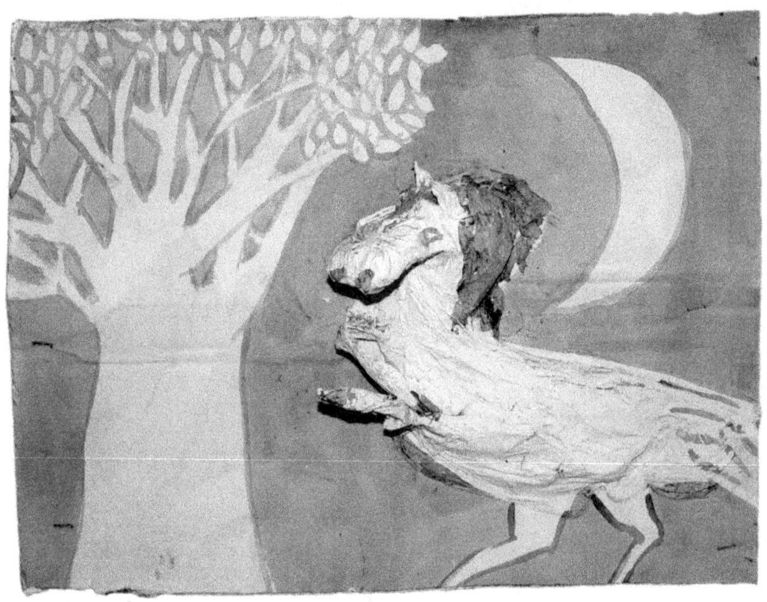

NY, and started school that fall, walking to the little country school with my cousins Patty and Jilly. It seemed like a long walk through the woods, which were often dark and a little scary. Soon we moved to New York City, where my father had work. But none of us spoke English except my father, and my mother definitely did not want to be back on a farm. And my father had to be in the city for his job. So we moved to New York City, and lived there all through the war.

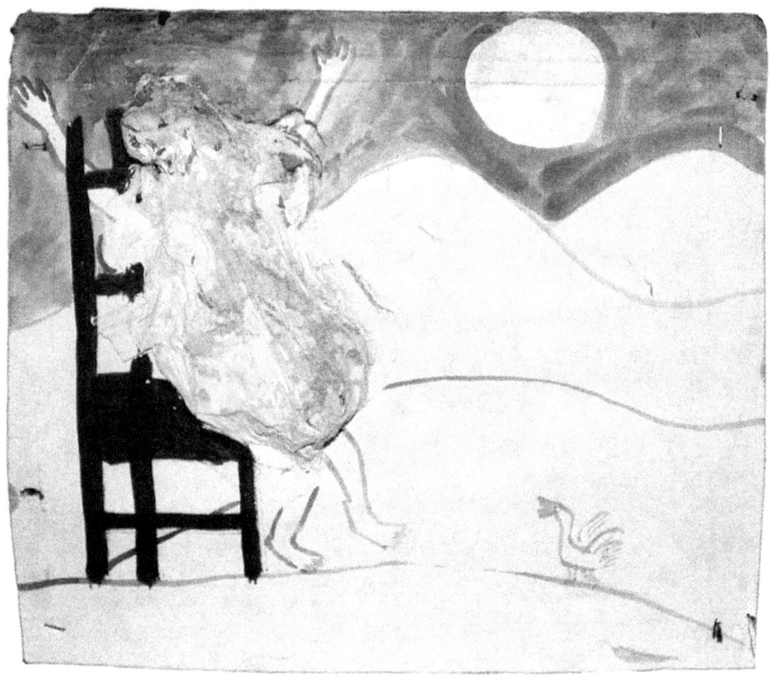

So I grew up basically in New York City near Washington Square. My sister and I went to school through 8th grade at City and Country School in Greenwich Village, a very wonderful independent school. Father wanted us to go to a public school because he very much believed in public schools. But then he kind of thought, since we didn't know English, a small private school would be better. It was a very progressive school with small classes and a different kind of way of teaching. Not regimented at all.

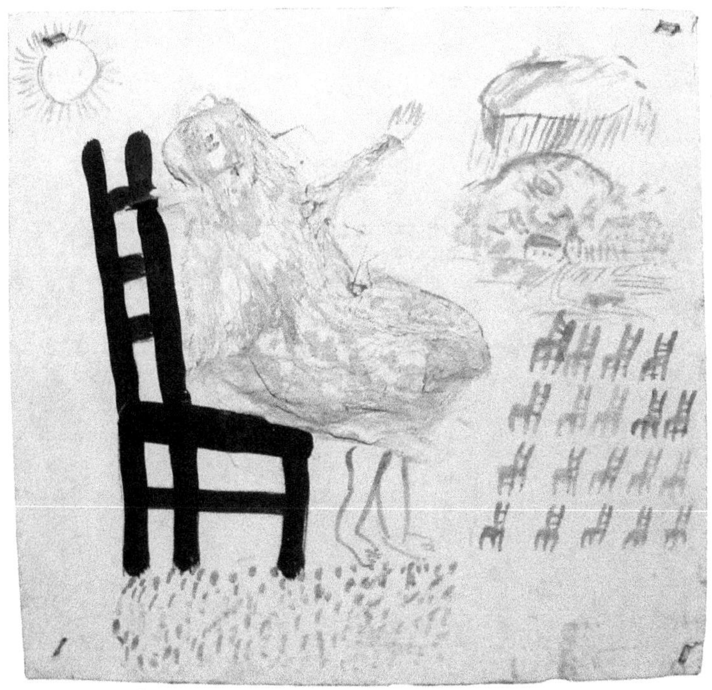

After the war, when I was twelve, my father was the head of the Berlin bureau for TIME and LIFE magazines, and we moved to Berlin. He wanted us to go to a German school, but then he thought, oh, you know, here we were in Germany as conquerors. That could make for an uncomfortable situation in a school room. So we went to the United States Army school for the children of soldiers with kids from all over the US. The kids were very patriotic to their state. And it was a good school.

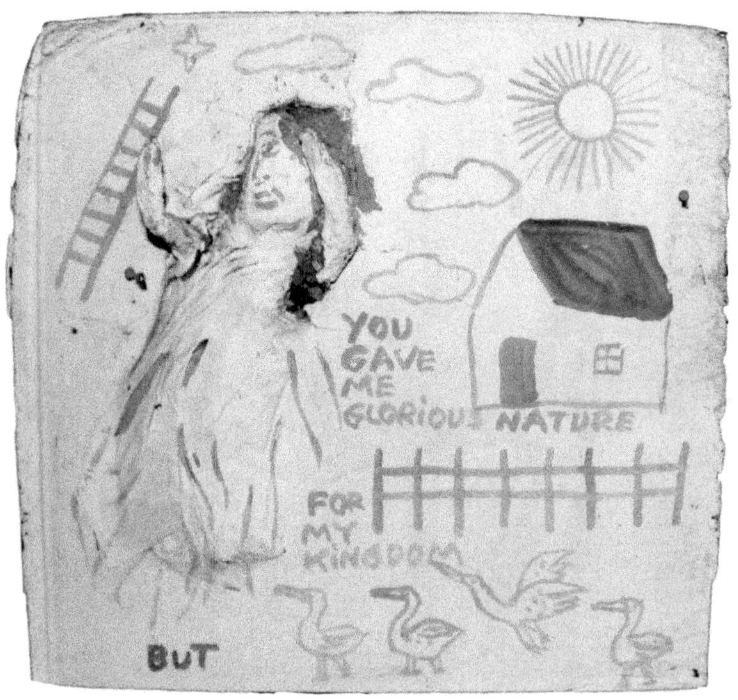

It was fun. We enjoyed it. And at home, English, American. But we had a German governess and everybody outside of the school that we dealt with was German. So I learned German well enough to then go spend a junior year abroad in Germany

At that age I think a child can just learn the language almost unconsciously. We sang a lot of German children's songs with our governess, and read simple stories, and very quickly we were talking, we could talk,

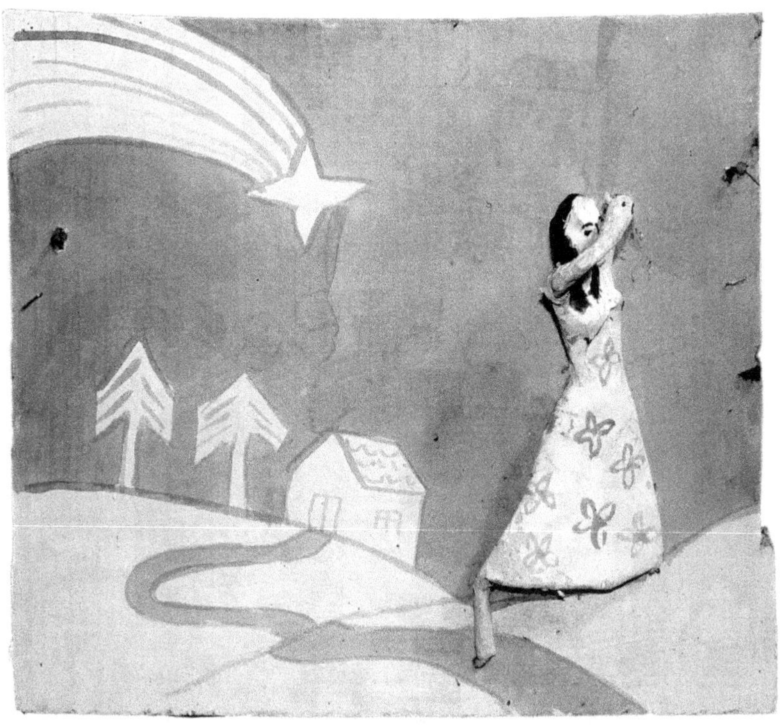

you know, baby German, kitchen German, or whatever. I never learned correct grammar. And I still don't know that. But we certainly could learn enough to get around.

My father was very talented linguistically. He had learned Russian when in Russia, and was fluent in German. We spoke Russian at home, but once in America, my mother buckled down and learned English, and ended up working on her PhD in English from NYU.

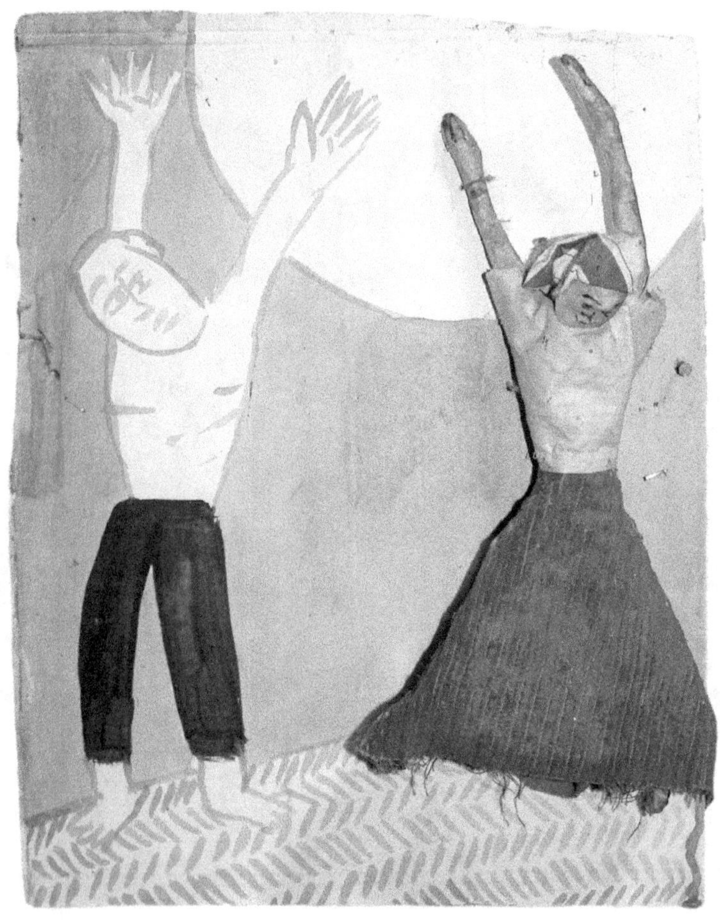

I had a very interesting childhood, but of course it was not my doing, and I can take no credit for it.

HIGH SCHOOL — During my high school years we lived in Ridgefield, CT. The political situation had changed so drastically over this period from the early 40s to forty-six or so. During the war, the U.S. and USSR were close allies, and all during the war I think my favorite games in school were pretending to be Russian guerrillas fighting the Nazis. And my

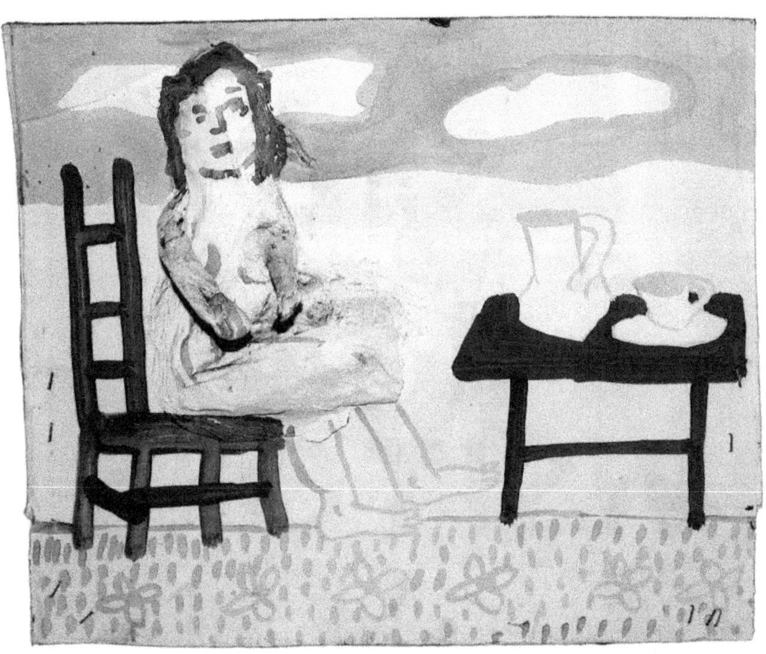

mother was very active in giving lectures about the Soviet Union and working for an organization called Russian War Relief, raising money to send to this country that lost 20 million people in the course of the war. And all her family was there, of course, so for her, it was for sure an anxious time knowing that Nazi armies just ran over the village where she lived, ran over a huge portion of European Russia at first. But still, the whole atmosphere, I was very proud of being Russian and fighting the Nazis.

SHE HAS VISITORS

And then in the end, when we were in Berlin, in the school, it was almost overnight. Suddenly, suddenly, it was like, you know, people pointing fingers at kids, pointing fingers at me and say, oh, you're a commie, you're a commie, you know, like in New York. And also, the first year of being in Berlin, the allies, this friendship was still quite strong. And my parents went to a lot of parties and receptions and so on with Russian generals, French, you know. Berlin was divided into four sectors, French, Russian,

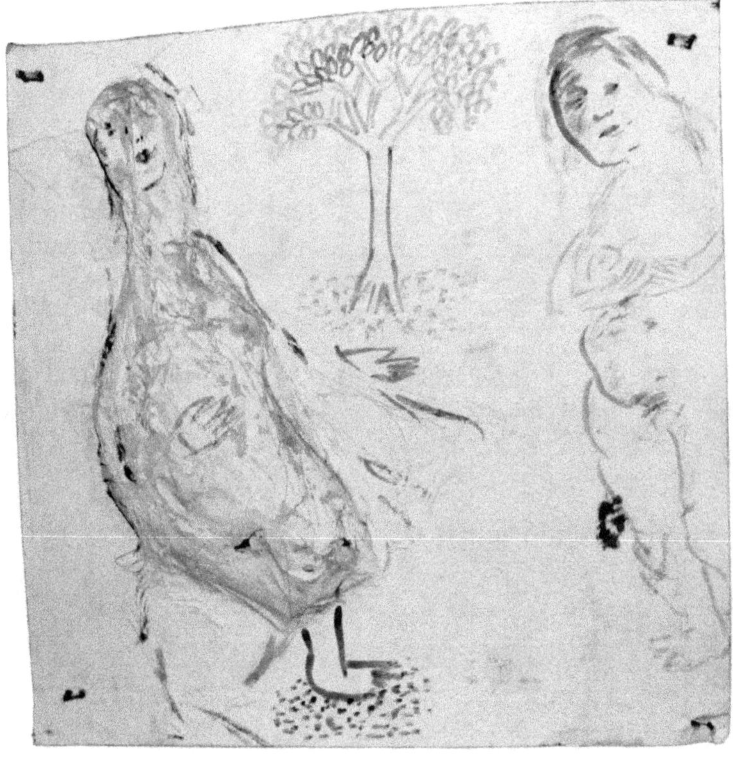

English and American. And there were a lot of parties and balls and everything. My mother had very fancy dresses to go to these places. But again, things began to get tense. And the Russians were regarded as an enemy.

My father, inspired by his father's building skills, built our home in Ridgefield—a magnificent four-story stone building, with all the wood and stone coming off our land. I was a student at Ridgefield High, an average American public high school. It was the beginning of the Cold

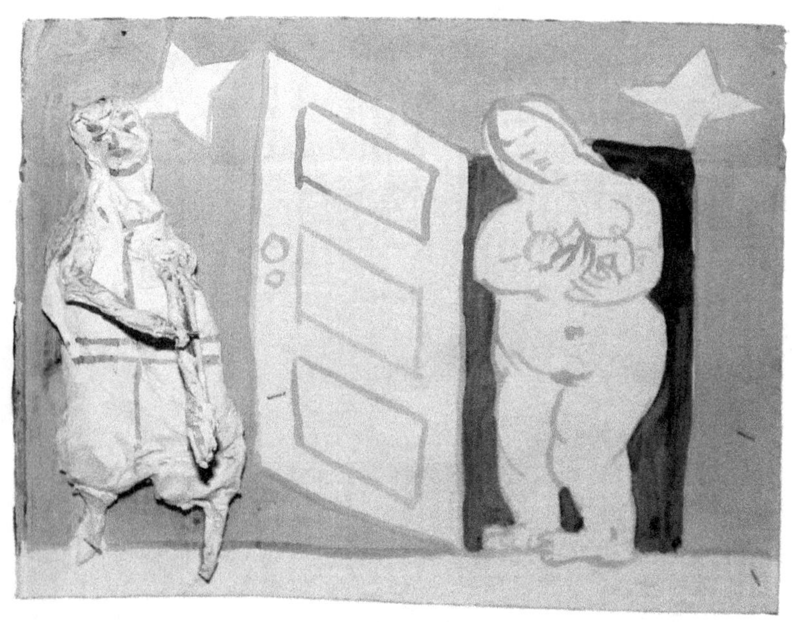

War, and I was very aware of my Russian side. I remember my mother would cringe when she heard anti-Soviet comments. I was angered when one of my teachers was discussing Slavic languages and said that "Slav" meant slave in Russian—I knew that was not true, that in fact it meant "glory." I wrote a letter to the editor of the local paper to set the record straight. But for much of the time, I was more concerned about how high I should pull up my bobby socks.

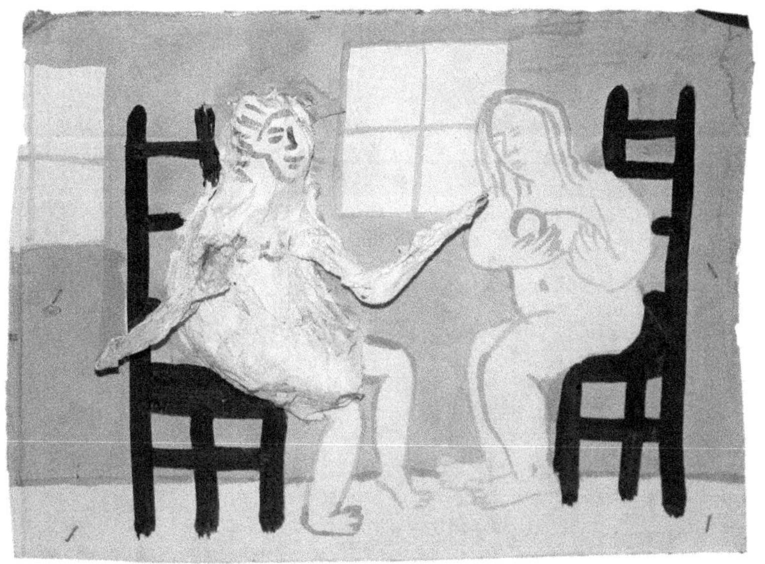

When he was a young man, my father had legally dropped the Nearing part of his name, to avoid being seen as just his father's progeny. My grandfather Scott Nearing was pretty well-known, first as a professor at the University of Pennsylvania in the Wharton School, and then at other universities. He taught history and economics and was very, very left wing—Socialist, a Marxist, I guess. He gave speeches around the country, and was very popular and got big crowds, once almost filling Carnegie

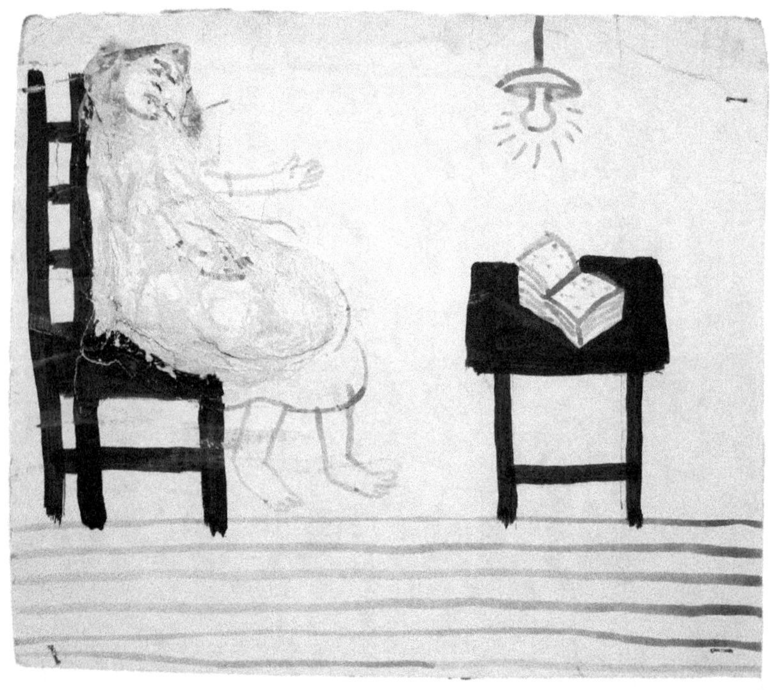

Hall for a debate with Bertrand Russell: "Can the Soviet Idea take Hold of America, England and France?" He ran for some political office, but he didn't make it. Eventually he was fired from the University of Pennsylvania, because of his stance against the 1st World War, and then moved to Detroit University. He wrote a book called "The Great Madness," about that war. Because he had preached against the war, he was prosecuted for treason, and put on trial, but he was exonerated. But then he fell into disfavor

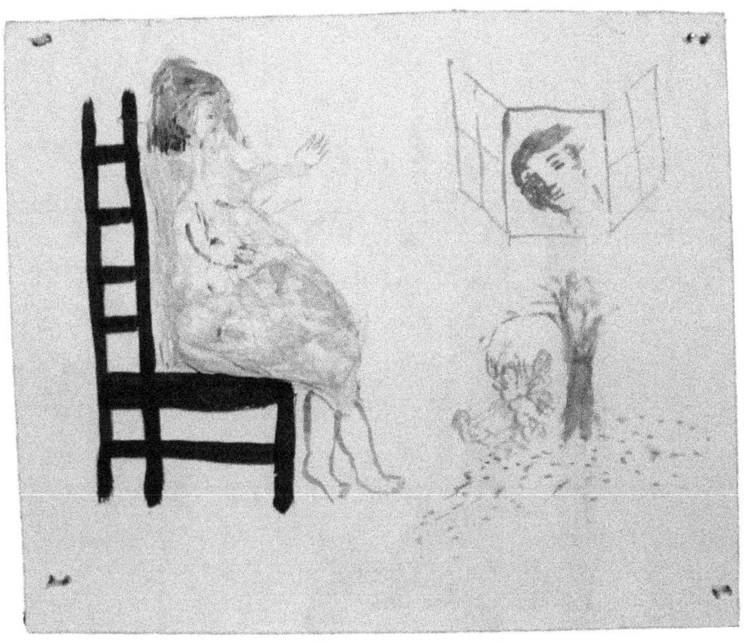

and decided at a certain point to move to the country and get away from the city and the pressures of being a public figure. He still continued to give speeches and lectures, but to ever smaller crowds. He had his passport taken away by the US government. He ended up in southern Vermont, in Jamaica, with Helen Nearing, his second wife. His ideas and lifestyle were a big influence on me throughout my life — living simply, back to the land, having a garden... The garden was very important. We often would

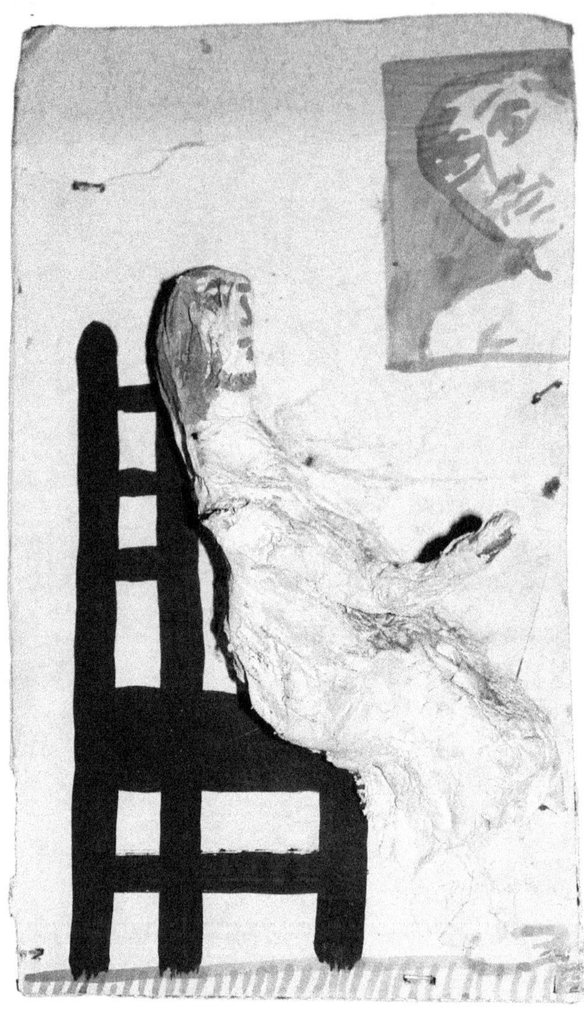

come at sugaring time, so sugaring was familiar to us. There was a community there, even though a lot of neighbors criticized him. He ate with chopsticks. Who ever heard of that? And Vermonters at that time were very conservative. But there was also kind of a community of other war resisters, conscientious objectors, who moved there.

Scott, in his books, when he describes his life, he wanted to start some kind of a, I don't know, in a way, a commune. He wanted to work

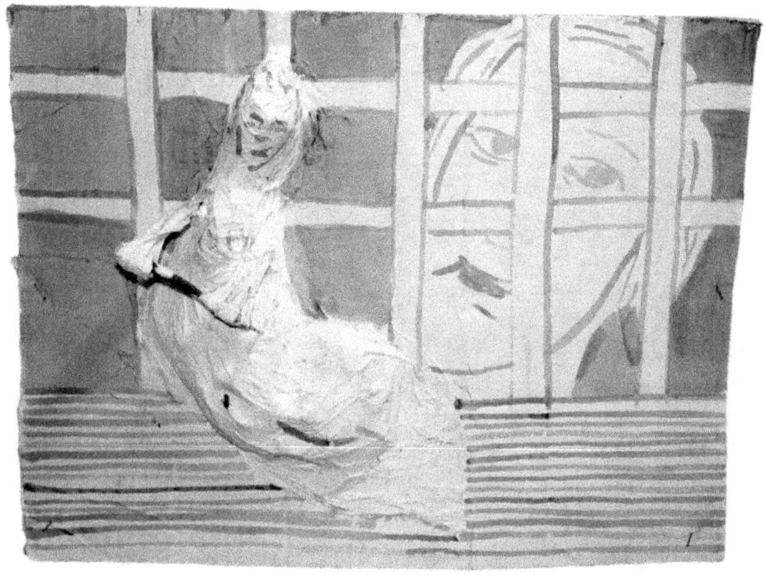

together with other people. But he was also very rigid in certain things that turned people off. For example, drinking. He was a complete tee-totaler and would not tolerate any kind of liquor in his house. And also anti-smoking. That was just part of life in America in the 40s, 50s. And he was very rigid. And then his vegetarianism… I mean, he didn't throw people out if they said they ate meat, but they certainly wouldn't serve anything with meat in it.

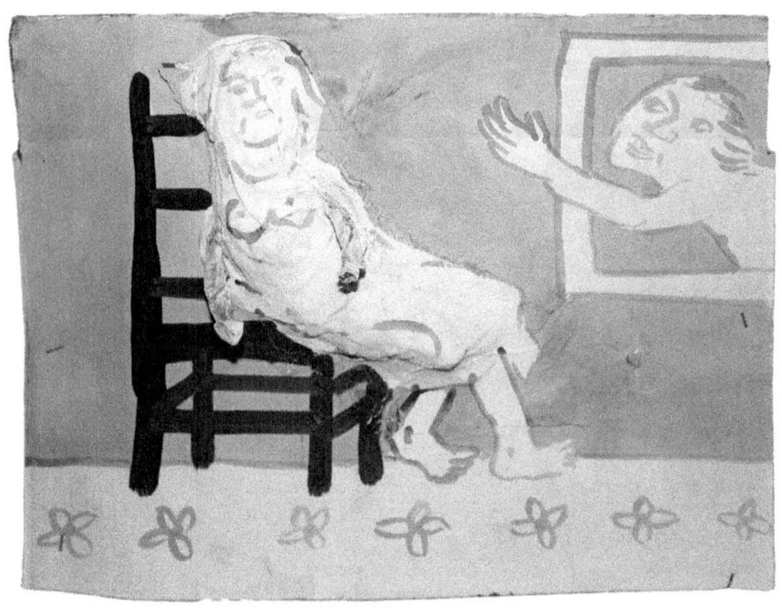

I remember when they visited us in New York, we had good lively conversations. I loved listening to the grown-ups talking politics, and then we'd ask questions. And when I was 16, Scott and Helen invited me to go with them to some kind of radical Congress or conference in Chicago. And I went there with them and attended the conference. But what I really remember was a tour which they arranged of the slaughterhouses, the giant meatpacking industry. The jungle. And that turned

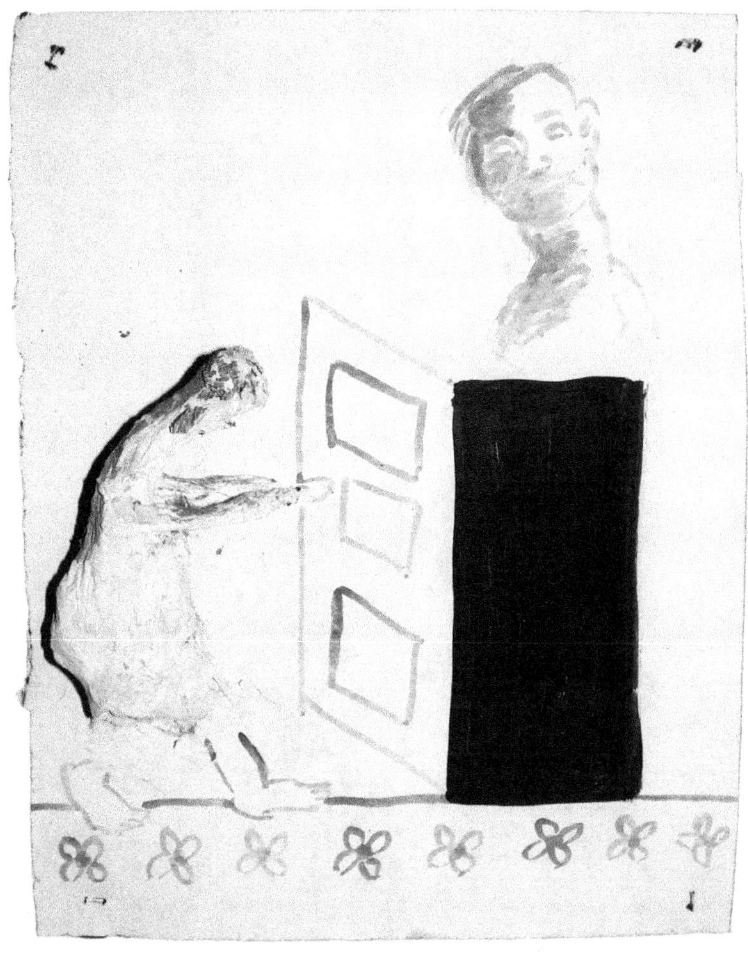

me at the age of 16 into a vegetarian for the next pretty much ten years. We all as a family visited them a couple of times a year. And then in the early 50s, Scott and Helen moved to Maine, and we'd make a yearly trip up there to visit. And I found out that their way of life, the simplicity of it, their wooden box, which we have now, very attractive. And, their conversation, again, it was so interesting.

I spoke out pretty early. I spoke out pretty freely and loudly. And I

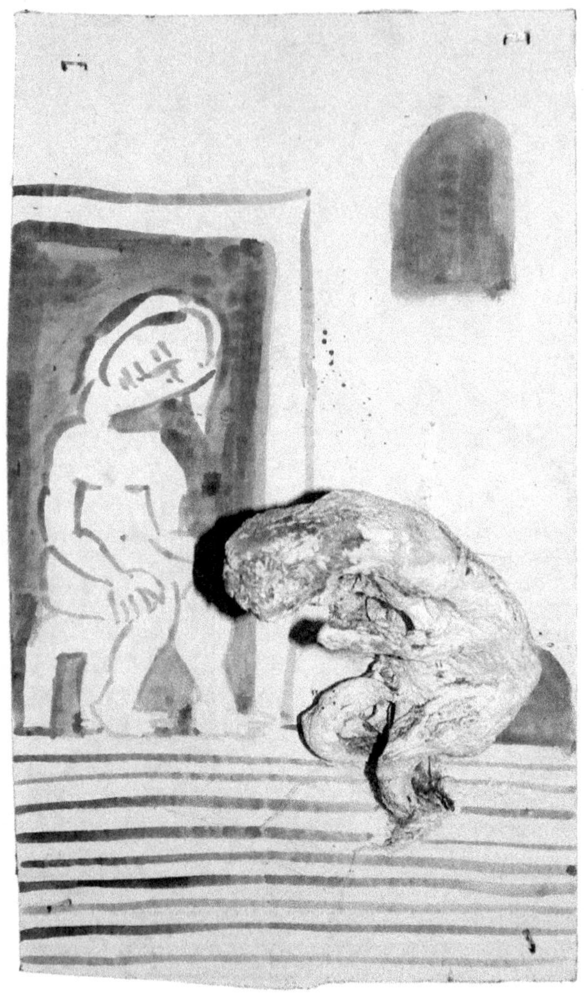

think one thing that put me in a bad light was a teacher in junior high asking the class who has books at home. And one boy raised his hand and said very proudly, We have books and we have five books at home. And I just was so disdainful of this. And I made it very clear how much superior I felt. And I'm sure that didn't win me too many friends or anything. I did have some odd friends, but I certainly wasn't part of the popular girls. I wanted to be, and I would try, you know, to turn my socks over just

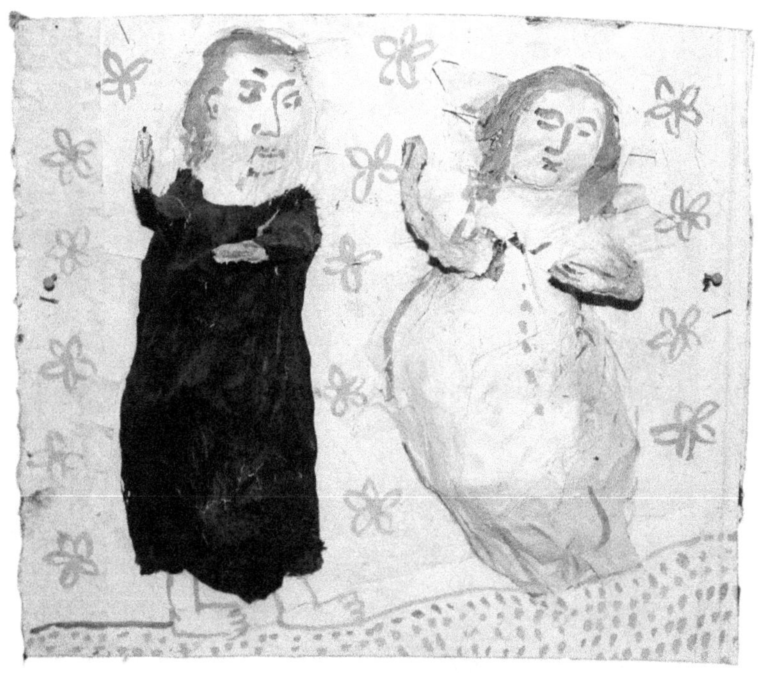

the way they did, and get a permanent wave and all these things. But it didn't help.

Scott gave a talk at the Putney School and wrote to us about it and said how impressed he was by the school, by the students, how open-minded and curious they were, what good questions they asked. So he really made me aware of that place. But mostly Scott's praise of the Putney School made me think maybe I could go there for my senior year.

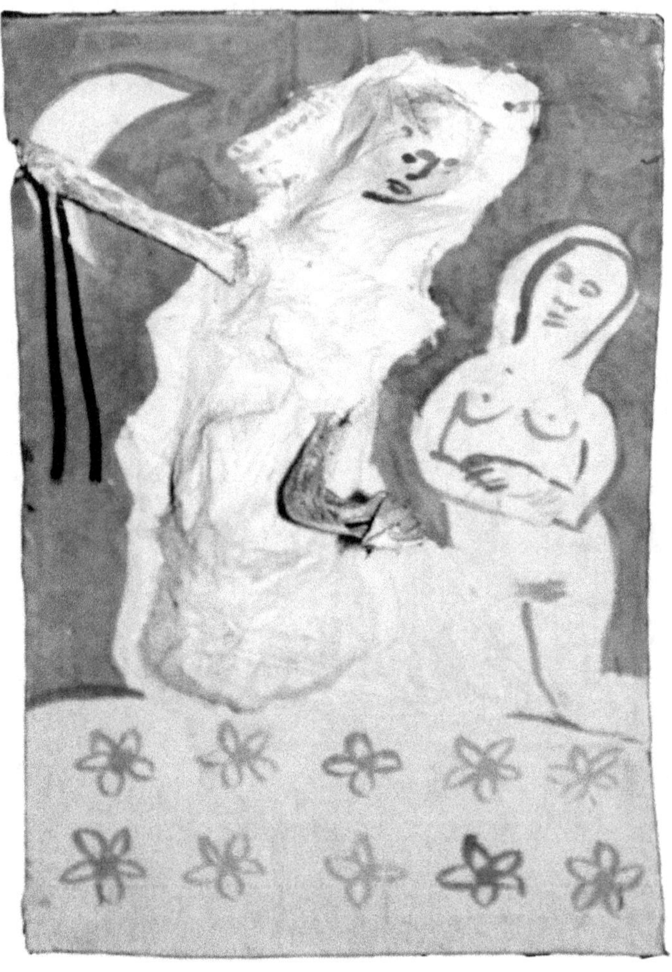

And I applied and was accepted and I went there for my last year in high school. And that was certainly a very mind-opening thing. And southern Vermont and with the emphasis on gardening, agriculture, the barn, the cows, the, you know, work ethic and all that, and music. Music was so good and it seemed fun to do that.

COLLEGE — I went to college at Bryn Mawr, where my grand-mother Nellie Seeds, Scott Nearing's first wife, was an alumna. I thought

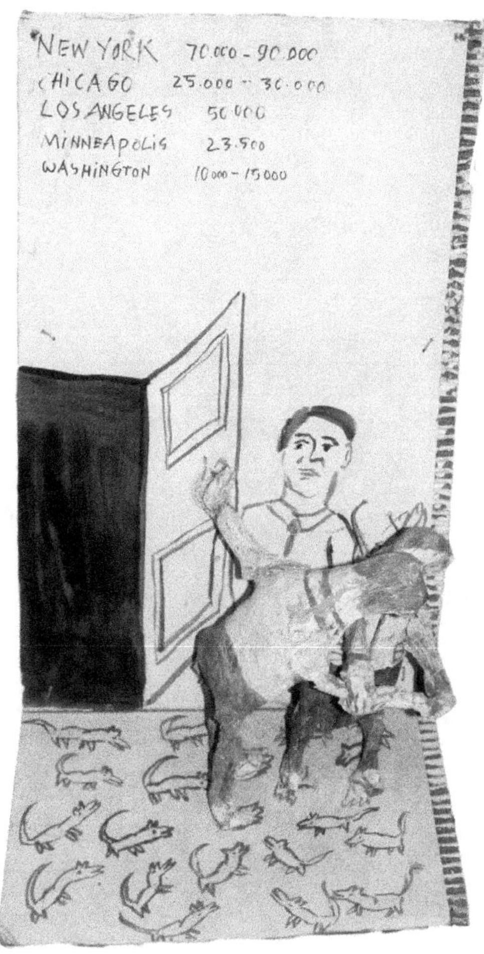

I might have a better chance of a scholarship there. I went there and right away I got very disappointed because so many of the classes, the girls were so demure and just taking notes and not asking questions and knitting argyle socks for their boyfriends the whole class. I just was quite disappointed. It seemed very narrow and boring or something. But then at the end of the year, I met a kind of another circle of young women who were not very ambitious, but were taking the train into Philadelphia

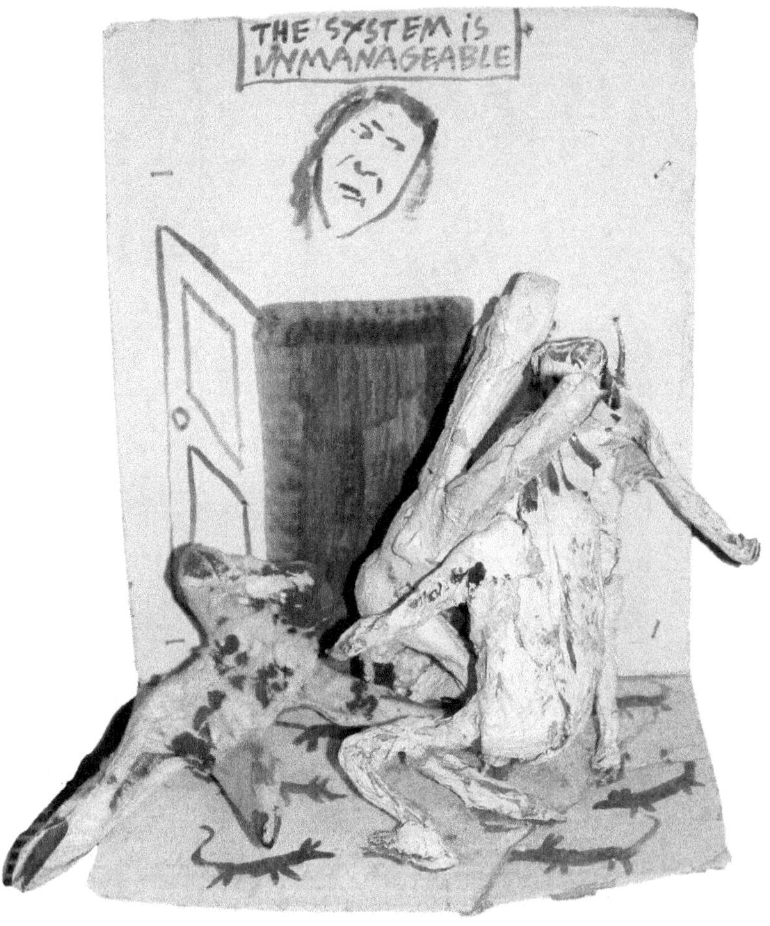

and joining Quaker groups that were going to poor housing places and helping people fix their houses and also to wonderful concerts in Philadelphia. But still, at the end of my sophomore year, I thought I have to quit school and work in a factory and be a worker, or change schools or something. And my father very much said, you know, you can always work in a factory. You get your degree first and then decide what to do. And then I thought of the junior year abroad program. I heard about

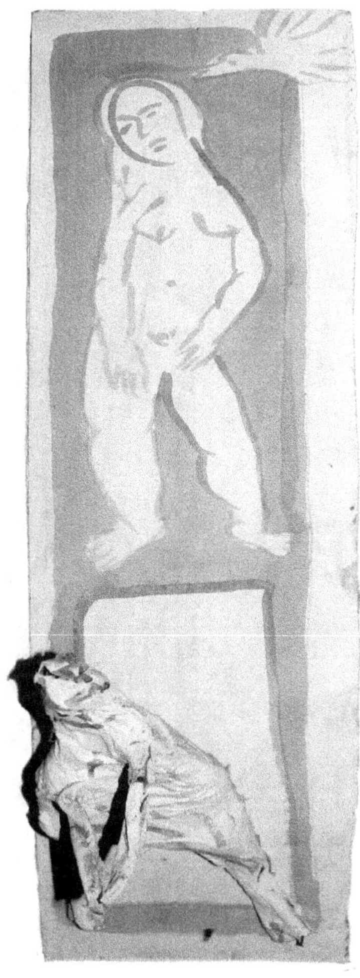

that. So because I knew German, I went to a junior year abroad Munich program run by Wayne State University.

I went there to study the History of Art, that was my major, and that is where I met Peter.

MEETING PETER — Peter was living in a sort of tree house. He was looking for people to begin a dance company with. His friend approached me on the street and said I looked like a dancer and asked

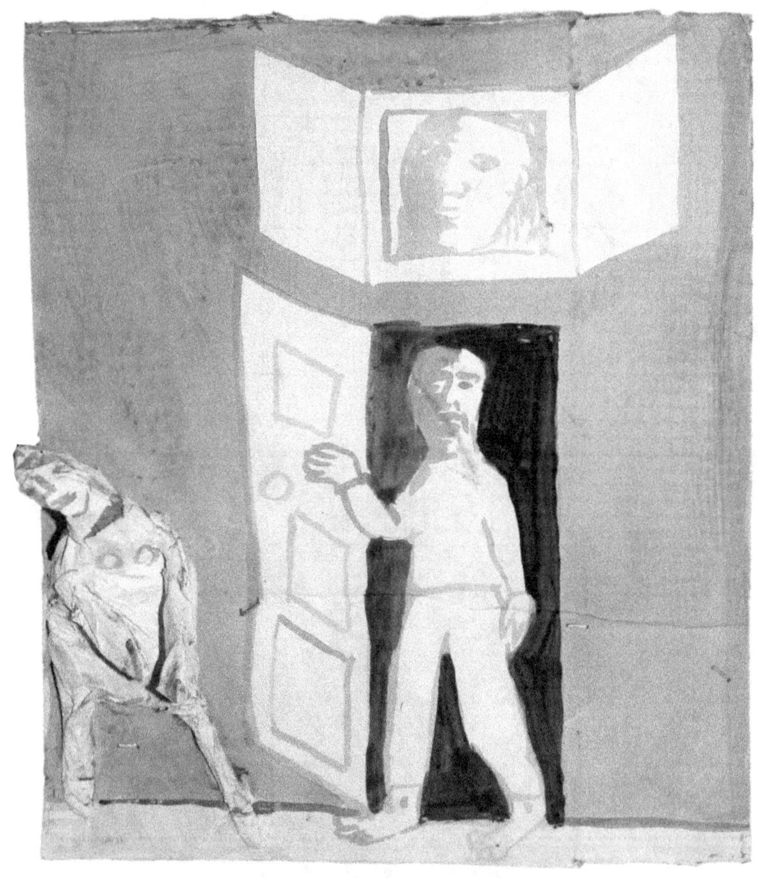

if I'd want to meet his very good friend who wanted to start this dance company. He talked about him in such glowing terms, you know, admiration and all, that I wanted to meet Peter.

Starting in high school, Peter had a vision of creating a new form of dance that was neither ballet, nor modern dance, nor folk dance, nor tap, or anything, but a dance that would consist of huge groups of people — many, many people together — performing very simple gestures, very

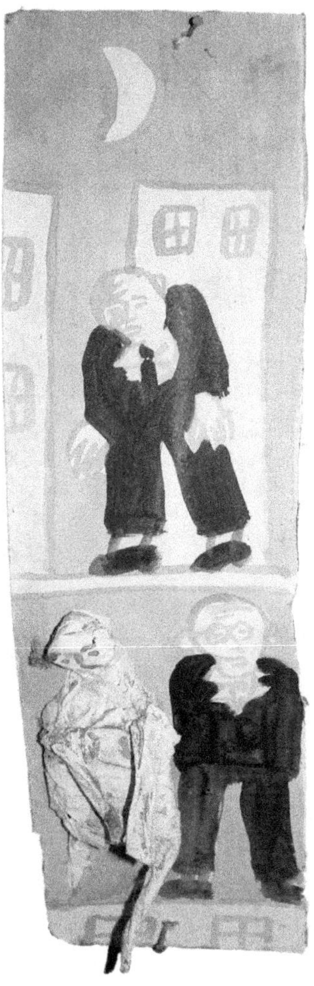

simple everyday movements: raising an arm, turning, taking a step or leaning over, but doing these movements with great concentration and power and seriousness.

But before I had a chance to meet Peter, he had an accident—he was hit by a motorcycle while riding his bicycle to meet Martin Buber. So suddenly he landed in the hospital. I went to the hospital, to just meet him, there, with his head all bandaged up. That's how we first met.

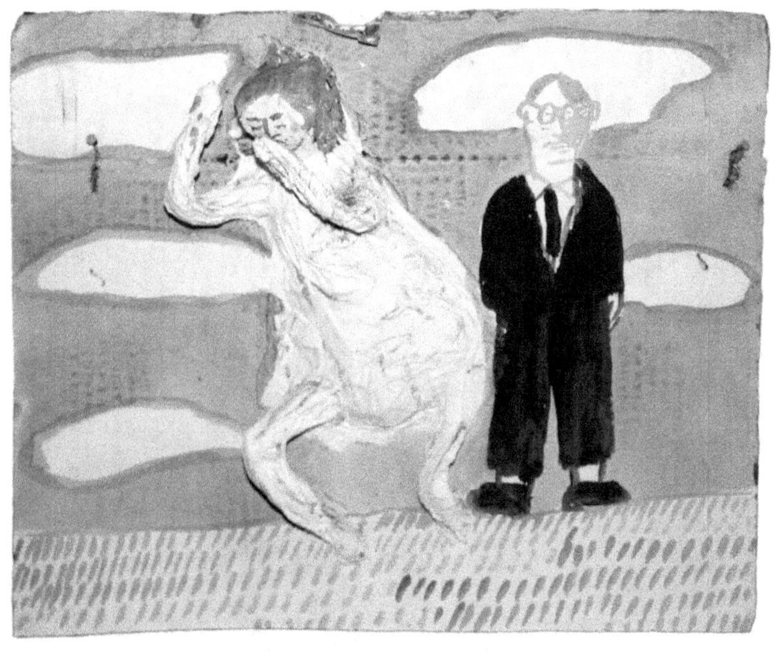

When I saw Peter in the hospital, he just made a huge impression on me. And I knew he was the one. It was like a mysterious thing that happens, that you read about in a good novel, and want to continue reading. Indeed, he was bandaged up and he didn't talk much or anything, but that's where it started. We didn't have any big conversations; he was still recovering. I just knew I had to see him again and again. It was mysterious and very strong.

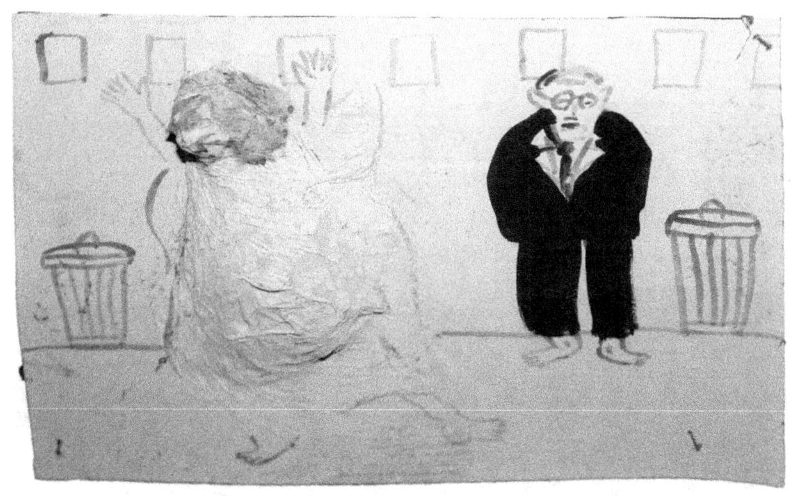

And after that we were together. Before my junior year abroad was over, I wanted very much to visit my mother's family in Russia. I went first to Moscow where I had cousins, and then to Udomlya, to see my grandparents. Then, back to Munich, where I was to meet my parents who were traveling in Europe, and sail back to the United States with them. But instead of getting on the ocean liner and going back to my senior year at Bryn Mawr, I decided to stay, much to my parents' shock,

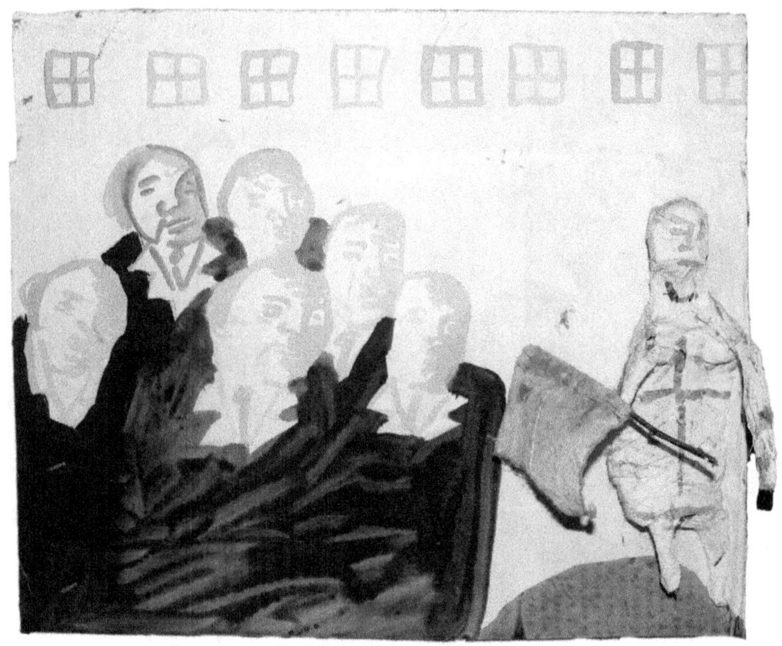

because I didn't tell them that I had met this man, and what was happening with me. I just stayed.

I hitchhiked around Europe a lot, even though I was studying, but the vacations in Munich were very long and very frequent because it was a Roman Catholic part of Germany, so they'd keep having saint's days and I would get on the road and go to Italy or France to look at cathedrals and museums and things like that. Peter was traveling around also,

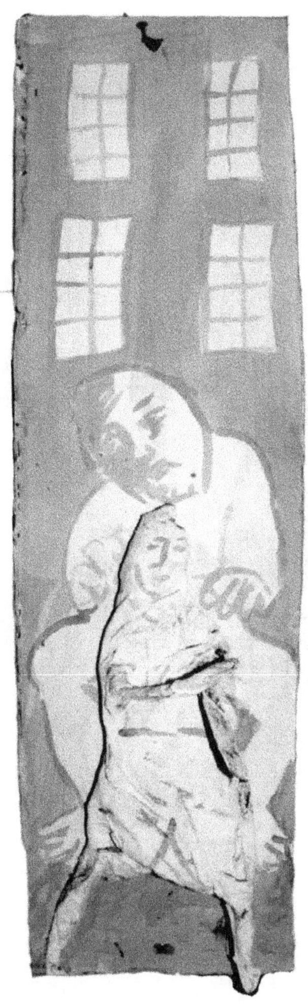

trying to find more people to create this new form of dance with. I wasn't part of it, I was sort of on the side lines. By the next school year, I had returned to America, and graduated from Bryn Mawr in '58, a year later than originally planned.

Then, it was back to Germany. And Peter. I thought of becoming a children's book illustrator or something. I was doing quite a lot of drawing and small paintings and things like that. Most of my high school and

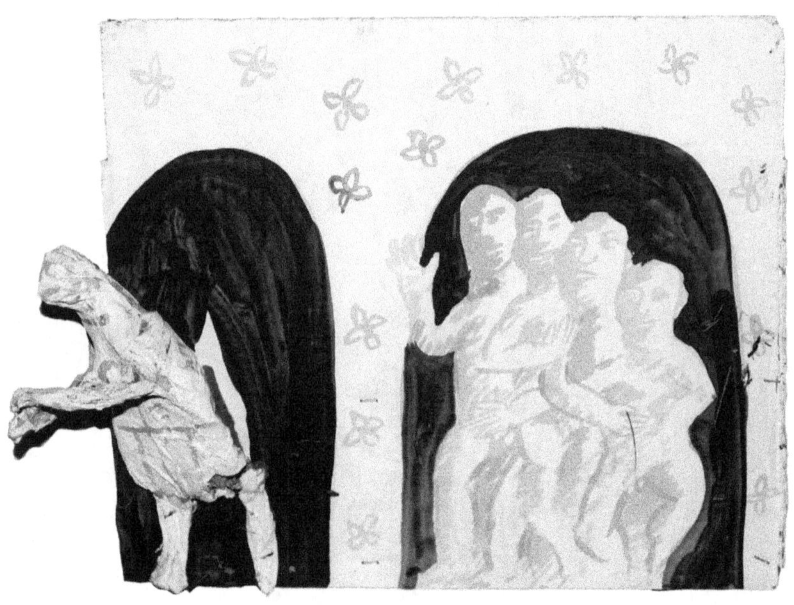

early college, I wanted to be a doctor. I wanted to help people, and be able to travel around to different places. But then after I went back to Germany, after I graduated, we very soon started a family.

START OF THEATER & FAMILY — We were trying to find a place to live in Germany, which was very difficult because in order to rent an apartment you had to be registered in the city where you wanted to live, and I couldn't get registered because I was pregnant and we weren't

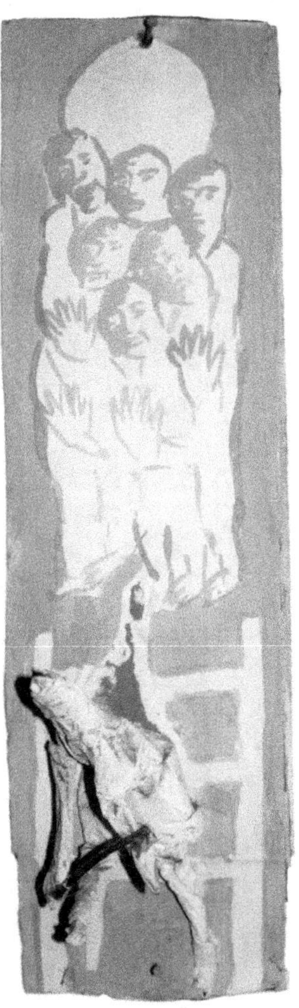

married and they were pretty strict about it, or made it feel that way. So we were going round and round to different apartments, and finally a very kind man offered us his place to live in a big house in the country-side. We were there until later we found a place near Munich, in a tiny village called Moosach, near a lake. The woods were full of mushrooms, which we collected faithfully. That's where Peter began to work with his dance company.

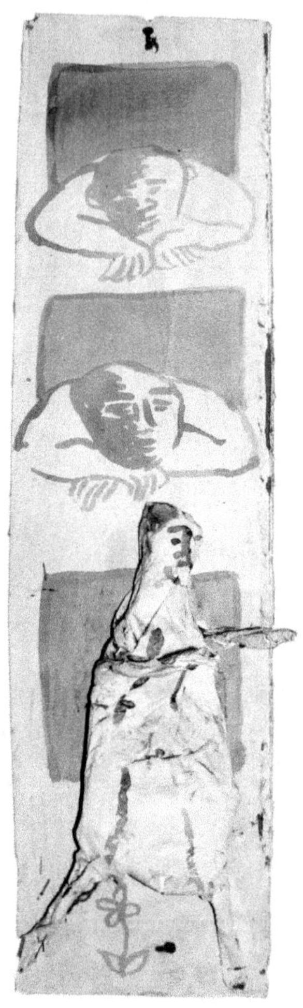

When we were in Germany, he was making over-life-sized figures out of chicken wire and putting papier mâché over a statue. That's a cheap way to make a big statue. And then he made a lot of masks and had the dancers with masks, especially the Totentanz, the Dance of Death, which was performed in the Judson Church in the very early 60s when there was no Bread & Puppet Theater. He was just a dancer.

One way we tried to support ourselves when we were living in in

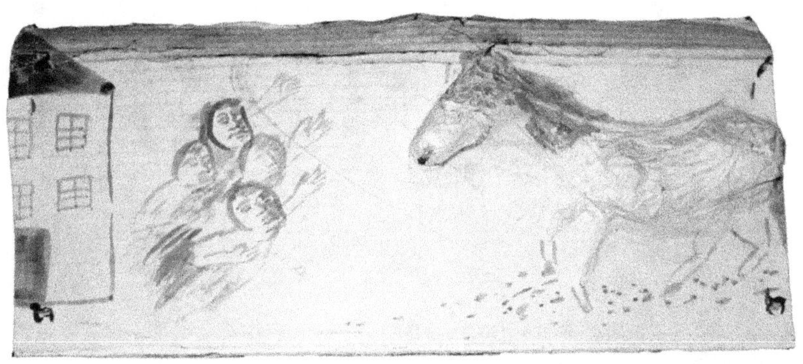

Germany — Peter would make these woodcuts. We even got expensive fabric, linen and things like that. We made prints on the fabric for wall hangings, bundled them into a rucksack, and then hitchhiked from town to town, going to the art galleries and trying to sell these things. I did it quite a lot and I never sold a single one. So then he went to art school and did sculpture there.

By that time we had one child, Tamar, and then another one shortly

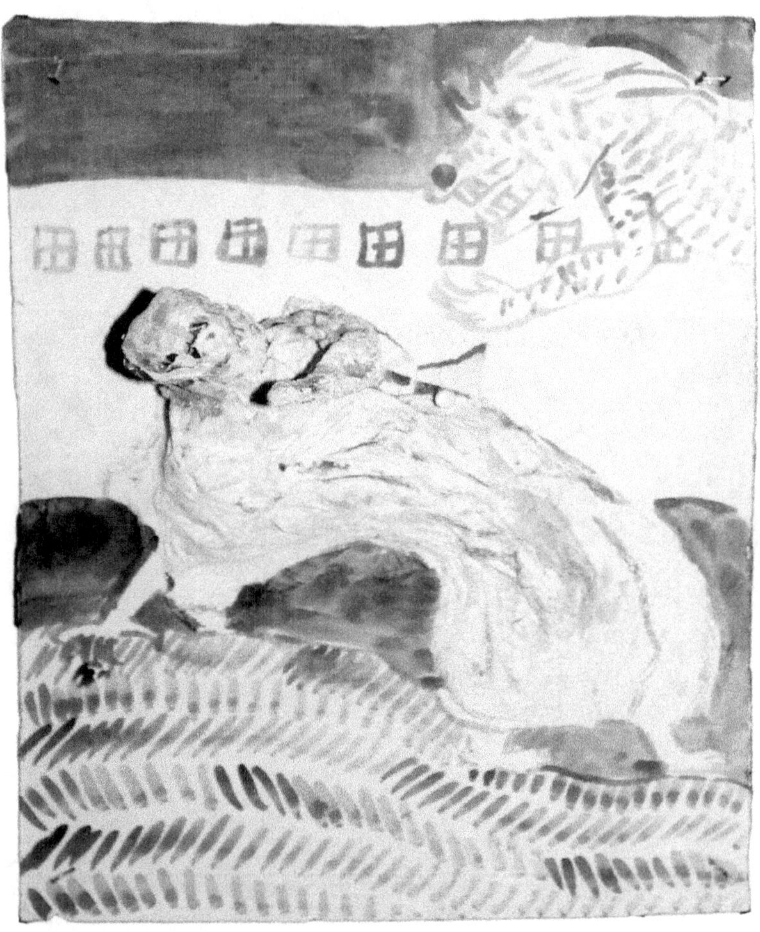

after, Ephraim, now called Salih. So I was pretty busy with that.

Then my parents invited us to visit, and we came to America thinking of it as a visit, but a long visit. And after Peter discovered New York, my parents were living in Ridgefield, Connecticut, and he started going to New York and making connections with the Living Theater and, avant garde theaters there, with artists and so on. I remember him saying clearly, "I can never work in America, I just don't know English well enough. I'll

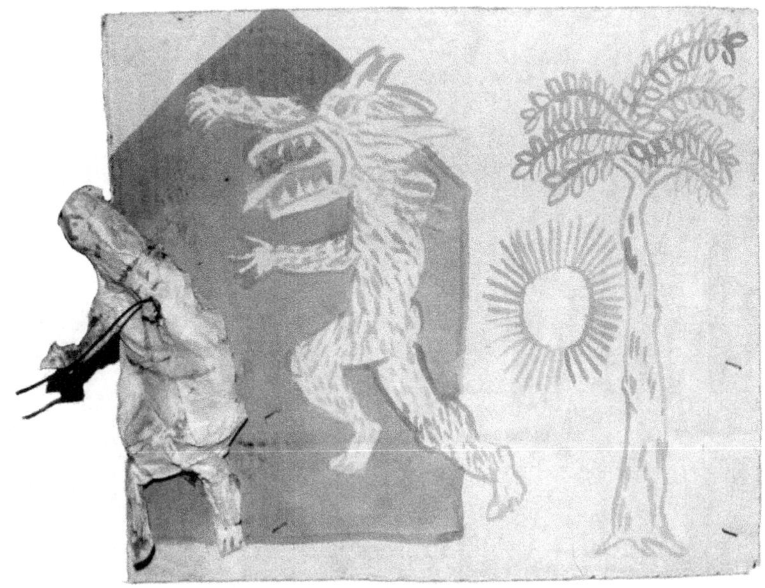

never be able to express myself." But we rented a small apartment in the Lower East Side and moved to the city. And then I think shortly after he got his green card so he could stay.

NEW YORK YEARS — In 1963, we moved to New York, and Peter started working, and got his studio on Delancey Street. Peter founded the Bread & Puppet Theater there. "Happenings" were happening all around us and then, in the early 60s already, the Vietnam War, that issue

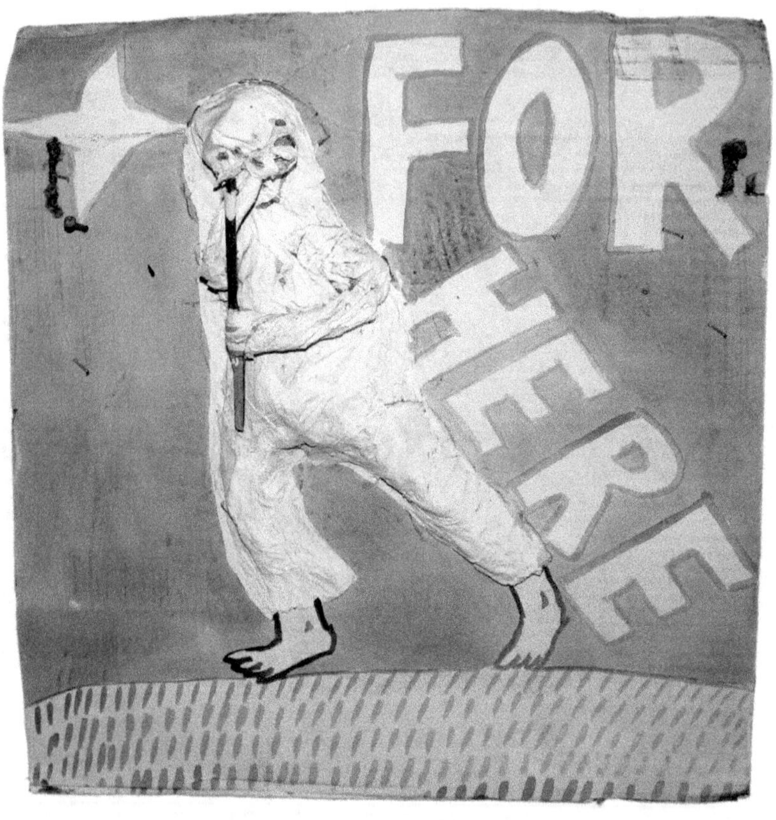

sounded a lot like it sounds now — like, oh, we're only helping our South Vietnamese friends against the bad North Vietnamese. We're sending advisers and observers... And then there was some battle and it became so obvious that the U.S. was heavily involved. And Peter took one of his big puppets, the Jesus puppet, and just put a sign on it saying Vietnam and just walked down the street with it for a while. And then the demonstrations started, the big ones, and he had puppets. And, you know, more

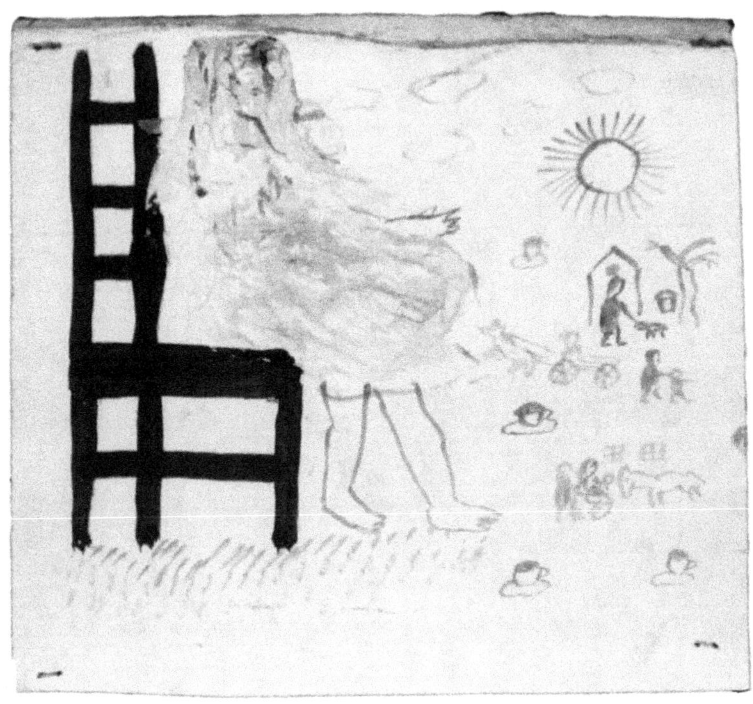

and more people were gathered around it, attracted to it. Expressing their feelings for peace and against the war in this much more active and creative way than holding a sign.

We built the first big puppets and we made shows there. I did some hand puppet shows for kids. But most of the time I was busy with the family. Then we had 3 more children, Solveig, Max and Maria. I didn't really start participating in the theater until we did a big tour of Europe

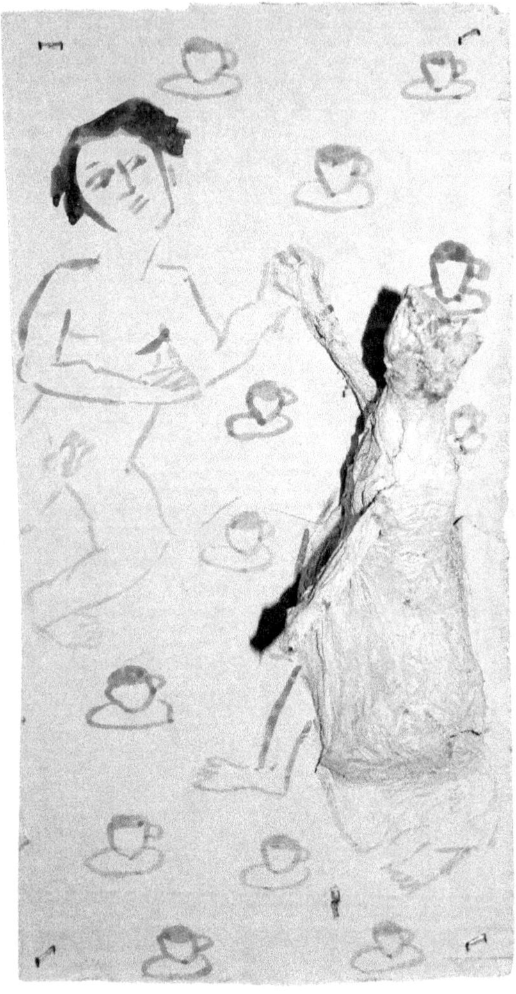

in the 1960s. I traveled along and watched the children. When we came back, I became the bookkeeper, the finance manager. I deposited the money from the tour and I took out payments for people's salaries. I'd make the same walk to the bank from our apartment on Delancey Street every Friday. One time I was followed home and mugged in the entrance to the apartment.

It was about that time we went to Putney School in Putney, VT.

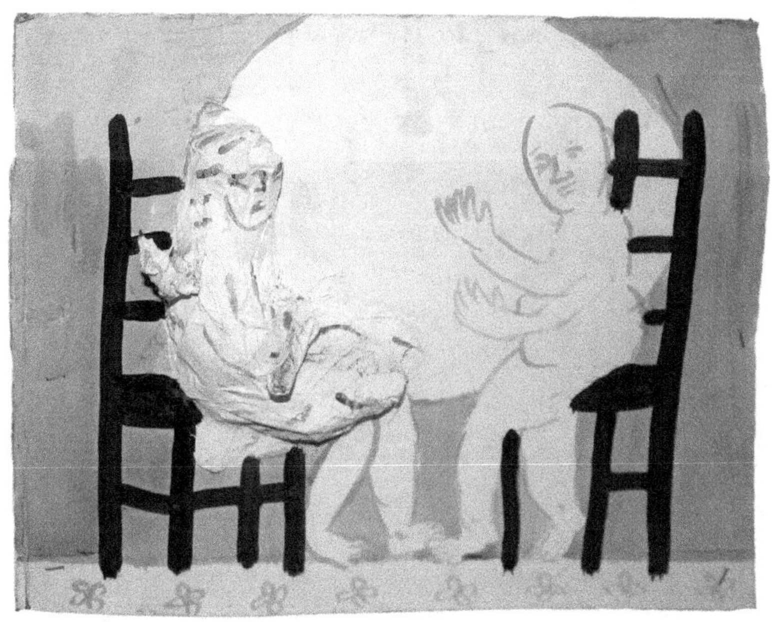

When we were living in New York, I was invited back to teach Russian because the Russian teacher, the one who was there when I was there, had taken a sabbatical. And it was exciting, I was teaching four years of Russian, my Russian was very good, but I didn't study grammar, so I didn't know of all the cases and verb forms and all that. I was staying up, burning the midnight oil, trying to keep ahead of my fourth year class. I did that in 62-63. And Peter applied to be the dance teacher at Putney.

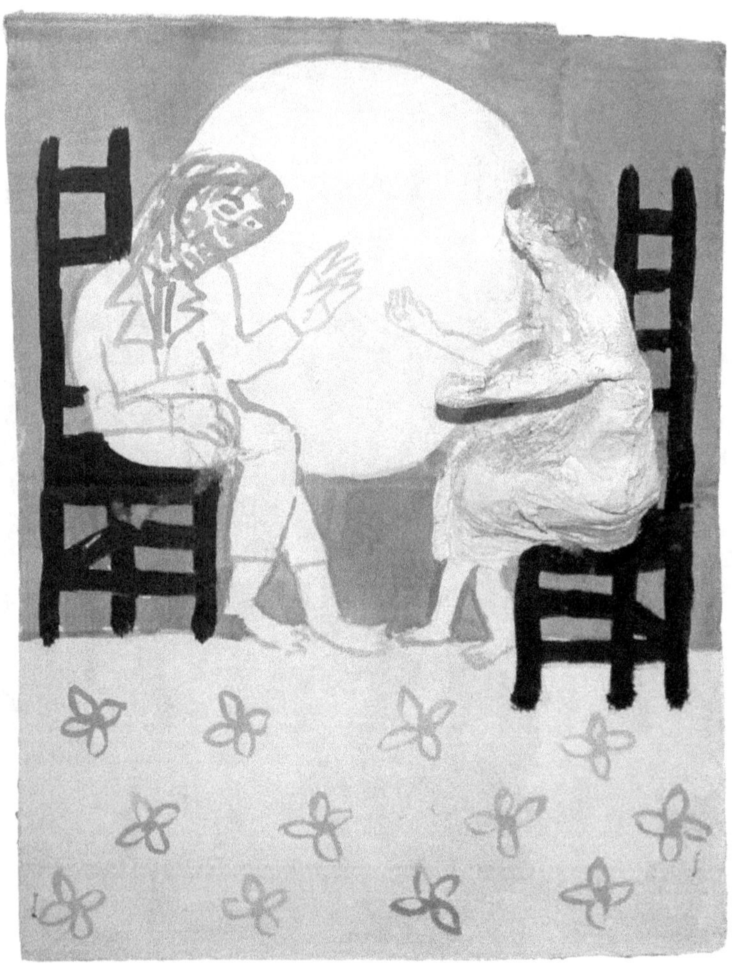

He invited them to come and see the Totentanz, the dance of death that was performed in the Judson Church. After they saw that they did not want to hire him. And so he said, OK, I can teach puppetry sort of off the top of his head. So he ran a puppetry class and I taught Russian.

After that, we went back to New York City. I was going to summer school three summers at Windham College in Putney. I was studying Russian and I got my masters there in Russian language, and that's thanks

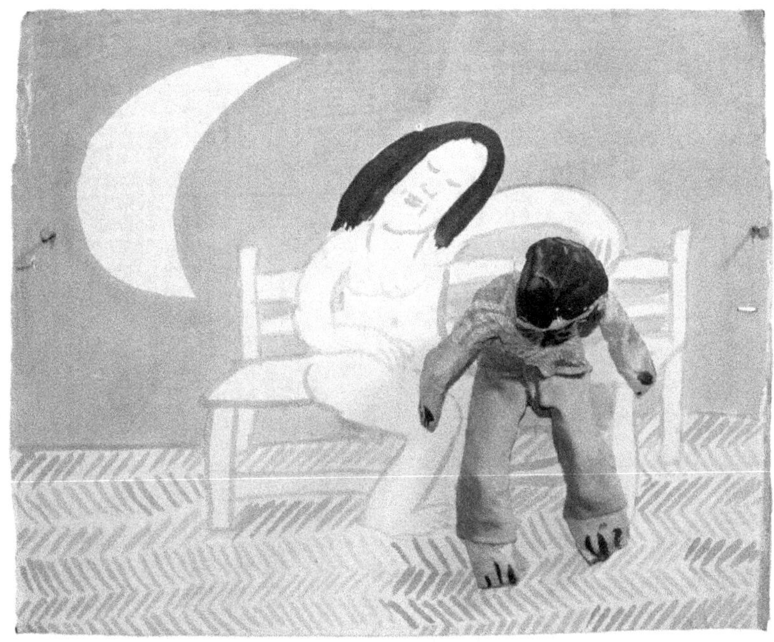

to my parents who supported us and helped me go there. My mother took the kids to Ridgefield for vacations. But I never did any teaching after that. I got more involved as the theater expanded. Peter made many different characters. I think I was maybe not the first washer-woman, but I was one of them. In the tours I'd be part of the performing company, and our kids also. The ones who were big enough would also join in and perform. We went on the very long tour in 1969 that lasted 9

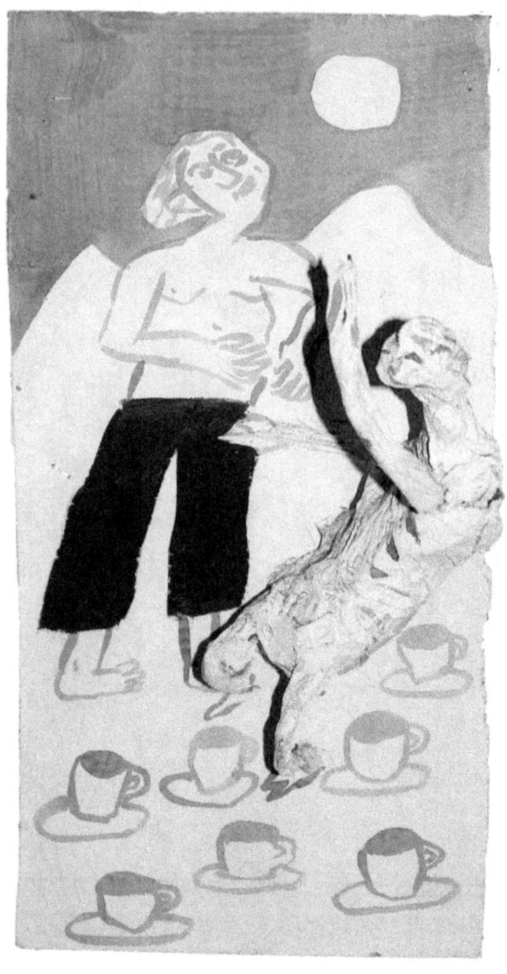

months, and then, in the mid-seventies, there was another big long tour that started in North Africa and traveled around the Mediterranean and Europe.

SEVENTIES/VIETNAM — At that time, just listening to the news coming from the radio, you got more and more aware and upset about what was going in Vietnam. There was all this talk about the US sending, not troops, but observers or people who were supposedly looking

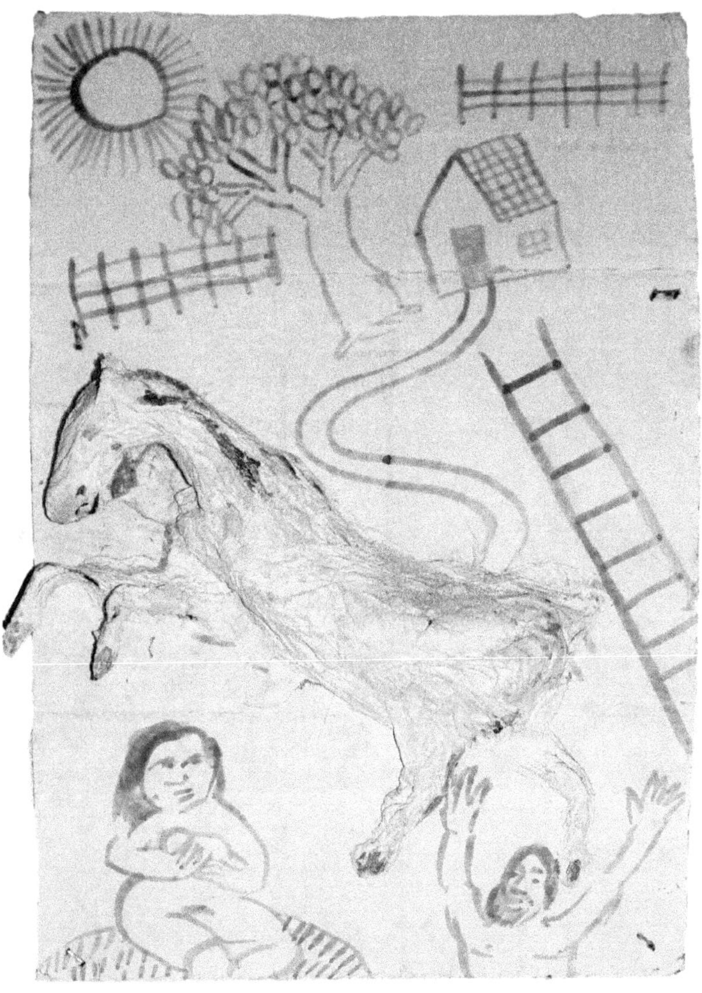

into things and advising, but you very quickly understood that they were participating in the war and becoming more and more involved. We got very upset about it, and Peter took the big puppets that he made and just carried them through the street, and I got a friend to beat on the drum and carry anti-war signs. The anti-war movement was growing so there were parades, and that was a chance to participate on a bigger scale and to really choreograph what was done in the parade. It was like a dance,

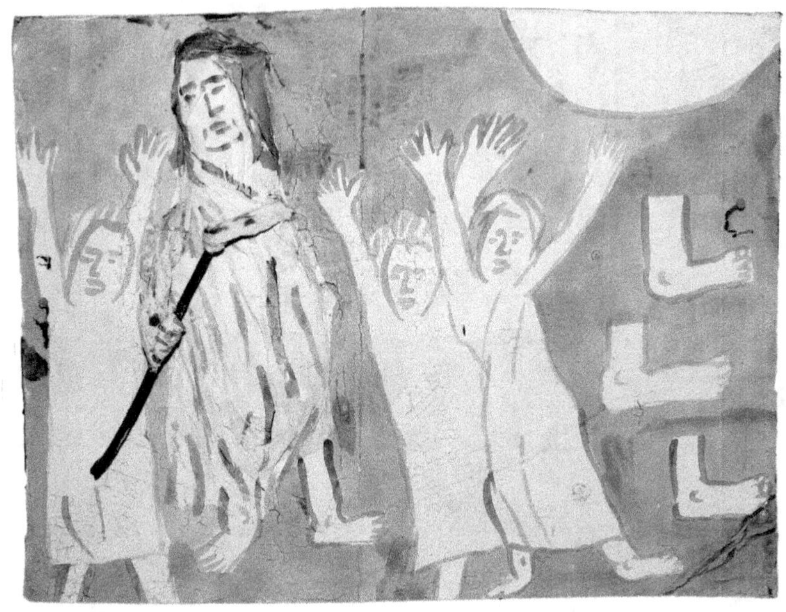

and there would be one contingent wearing skull masks and rattling tin cans and another contingent carrying white figures, blindfolded, portraying Vietnamese prisoners that would be attacked by this huge plane, the shark-face plane. There was so much activity. There were parades, demonstrations, marches, big gatherings in halls against the war and we participated in those. And they got bigger and bigger. We were completely involved.

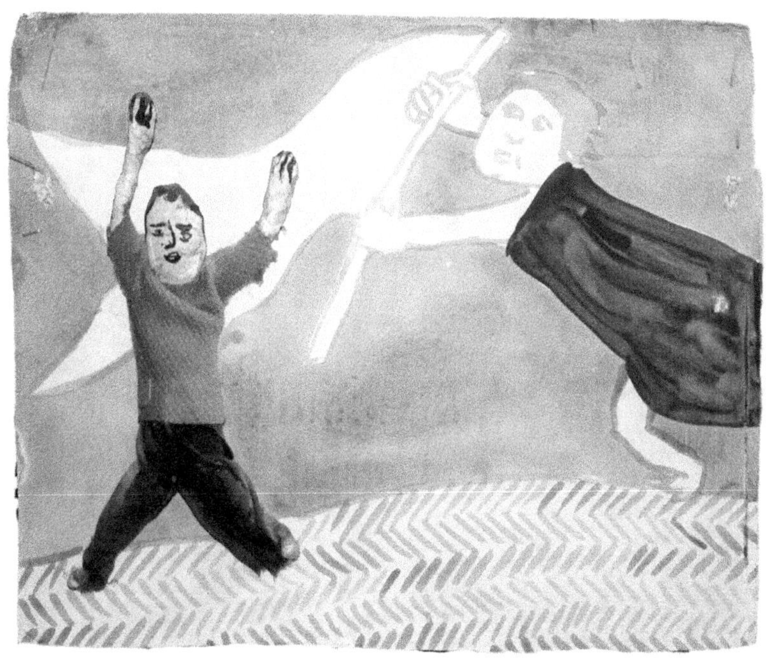

And in the city there was quite a lot of theft. You know, people's apartments are broken into, people mugged in the street. Our kids got knives pulled on them on the way to school and things like that. And I got mugged or robbed. Once, I went to the bank. I was in charge of the petty cash in the money. And I was picking up the salaries for the people who are working in the theater. I don't know what day of the week it was, but I would go out every two weeks. I would go to the bank and come back with

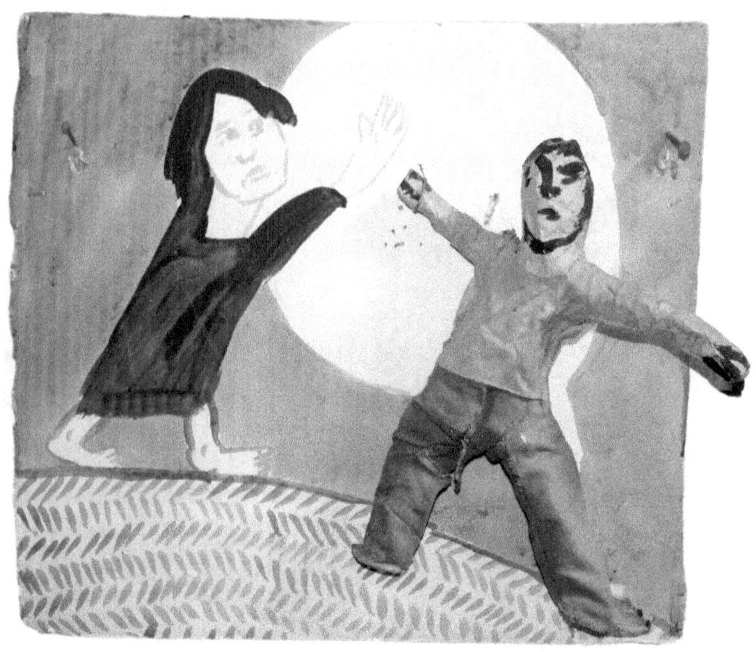

the money, and then it would be distributed. And I think somebody must have noticed somehow the regularity of it, because I came back from the bank, and right in our hall there are two men with guns, and they took all the money. And I was so scared. I was… I don't know. But we also at that time got the invitation from Goddard College to come. And so we were ready to. We were ready to move to the country. We had to find a bigger apartment. We really needed more room. We were ready.

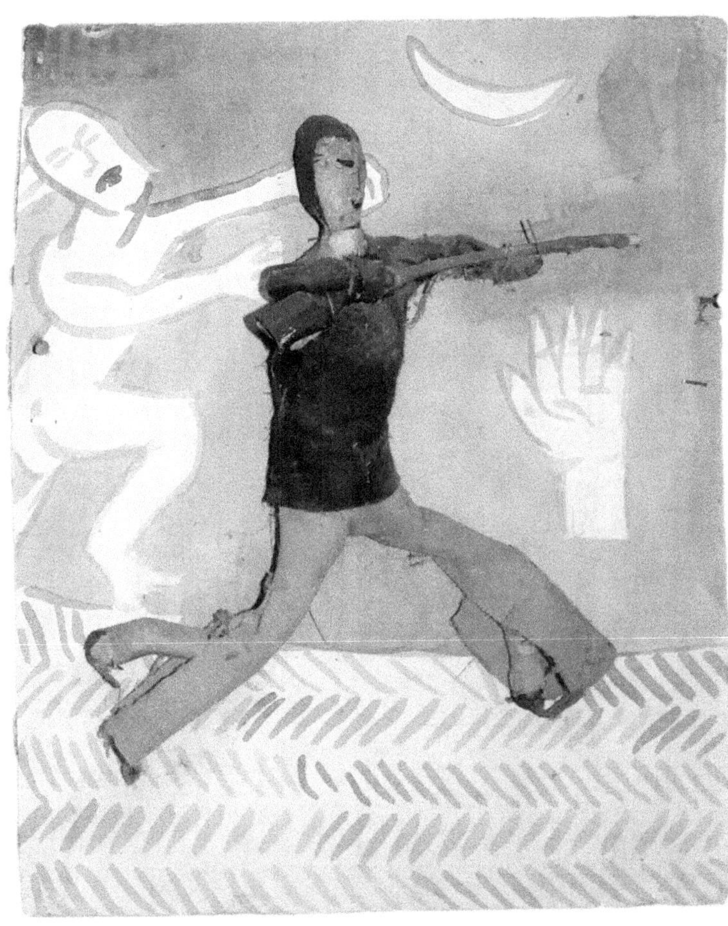

COMING TO VERMONT/CATE FARM — Peter and I both liked being in the country and having a garden and having the kids be able to run around outside, so when we got the invitation from Goddard College in Plainfield, VT, to be an artist in residence, it came at the right time and we were very happy to do the move. In New York, we were living in a very small railroad flat on 6th Street. The five kids were in one room facing the street in two bunk beds and a crib, we shared a hall

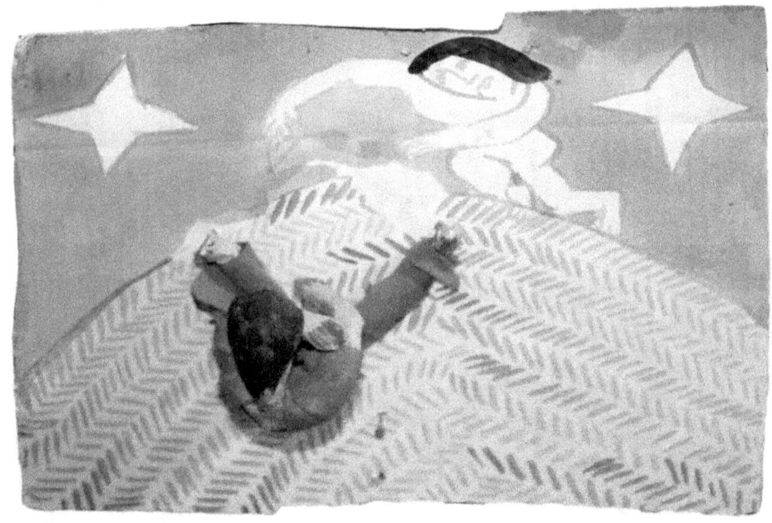

bathroom with the neighboring apartment and there was a small back-yard, that barely, barely fit them, so the idea of being in the country and having all this space was very, very appealing.

When we first moved to Vermont the kids were scared of the bugs. It was a big change, sort of traumatic, and changing schools was hard. They were going to the public schools in New York City, PS 122 and PS 9, and coming to a little country school where the kids already knew each

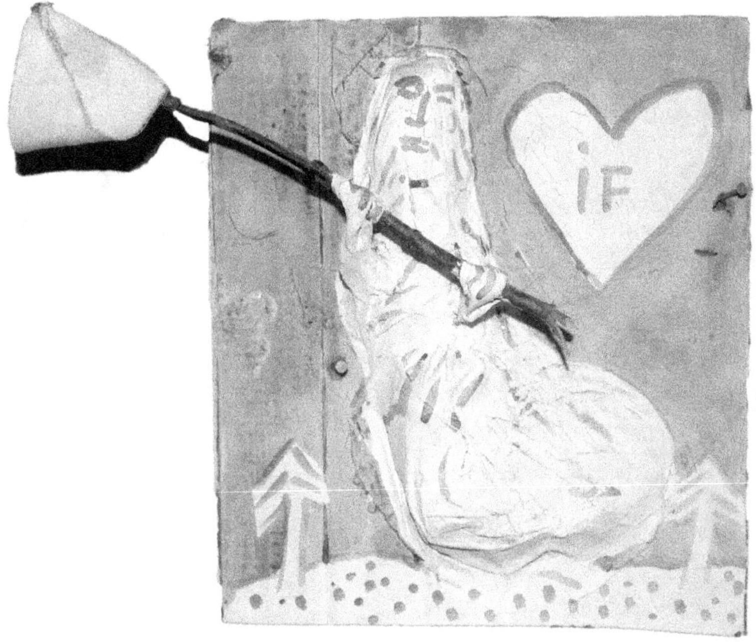

other and many of them belonged to the same families, that was kind of a hard move.

Living rent free at Cate Farm was part of the arrangement of coming to Goddard. We were given this beautiful, beautiful farm on the edge of a beautiful round meadow, on an arm of the Winooski River. There was a big barn with a small insulated section so you could work there in the winter, though the rehearsal part of the barn was ice-cold. We lived in the main

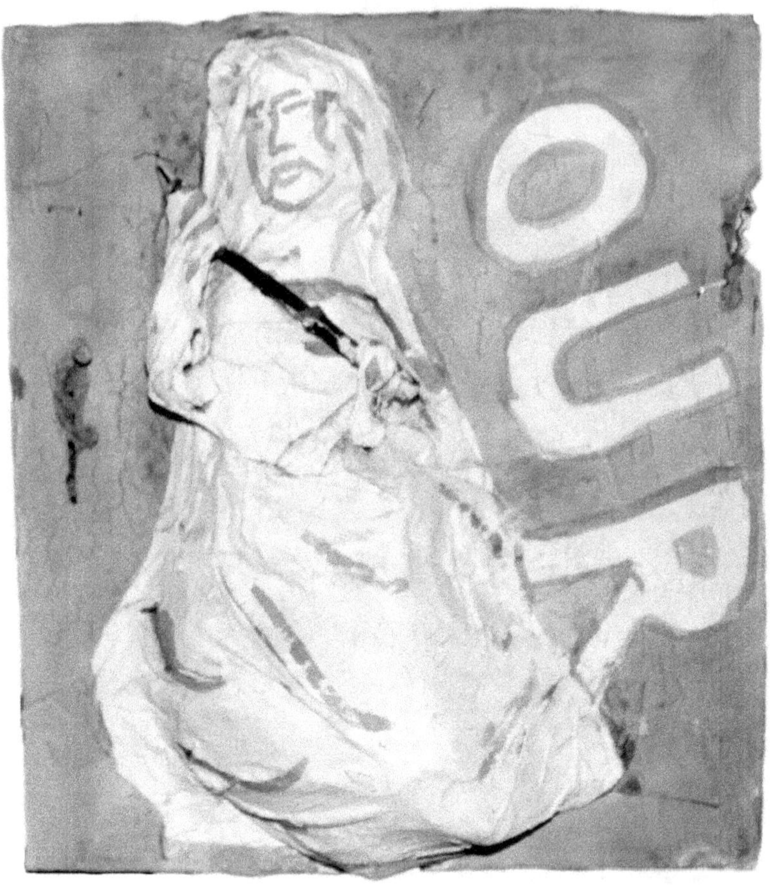

part of the old brick farmhouse, which had enough housing for a pretty big company then — 8, 10 people. The repairman from Goddard would come and fix the water pipes if they froze or broke, or things needed to be done. As part of the residency, we would always premiere any new shows in the Haybarn Theater and also work with students. Whoever wanted to work with us was welcome to do paper maché or be part of a chorus in a show or participate in street theater. We'd go up to the dorm areas where

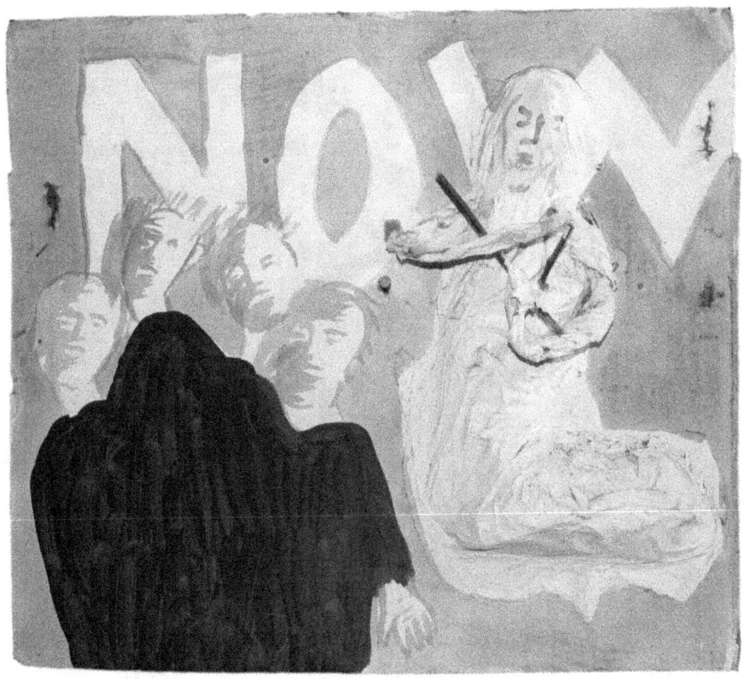

the student housing was and perform there. I had my own children' puppet theater, "The Dancing Bear Theater," there for a few years. We had puppets, and a trained bear who would do special tricks as part of the children's show act. We'd take mostly familiar fairy tales and poems and make them into puppet shows. We performed in the local schools and sometimes went a little further afield. That was fun to do, very satisfying with a few friends, and some of them became puppeteers with the company.

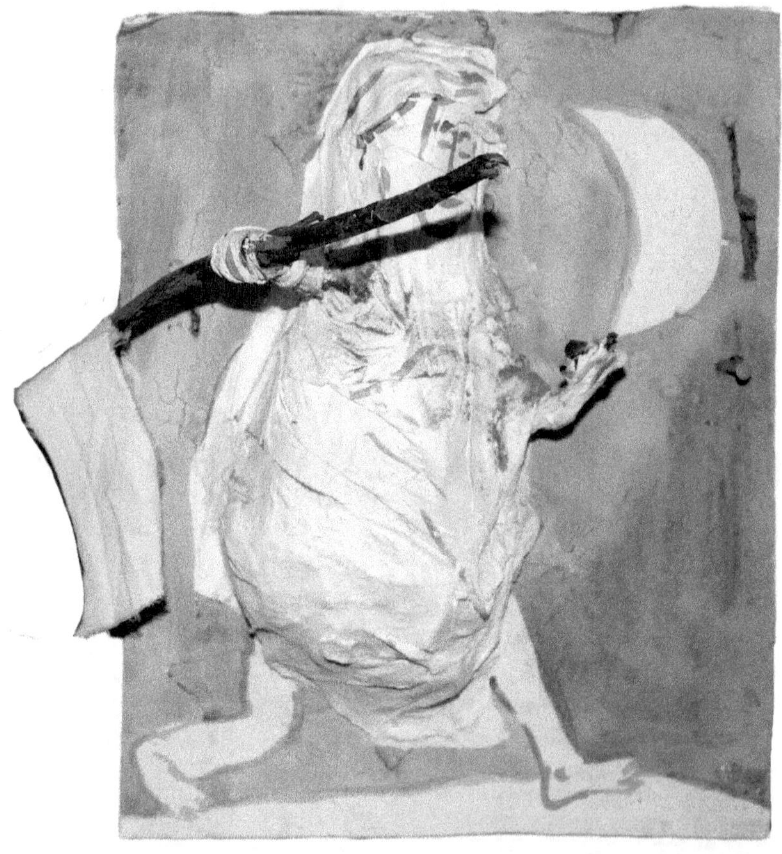

I had gotten tired of the haphazard and sometimes really impolite way Bread & Puppet would be in the public schools. They didn't understand that you should not come in with muddy feet or, you know, dirty, wearing dirty clothes, and come in late, or I don't know, all these things that a raggle-taggle 60s group of people would do. I decided I would start a children's theater that would come on time and be neat and take off our shoes before we went to the gym and do simple, cheerful children's theater. So I

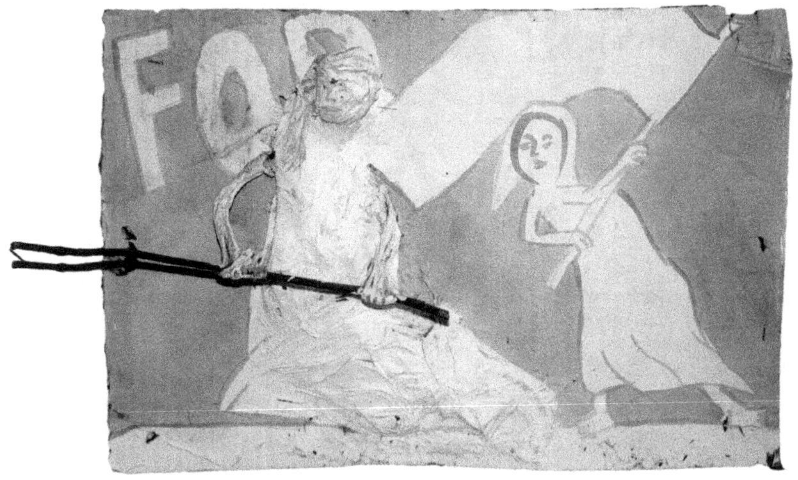

did that for several years, the Dancing Bear Theater, and I had a company of probably four people or so, and we did made-up nursery rhymes, and made them into shows, and took kids stories and did our version. I don't want to say clean version because the Bread & Puppet version was dirty. It was just more complicated, more political. So we did a children's version of the Christmas story that we played in schools. I guess that was before the school started being so strict about not having anything religious.

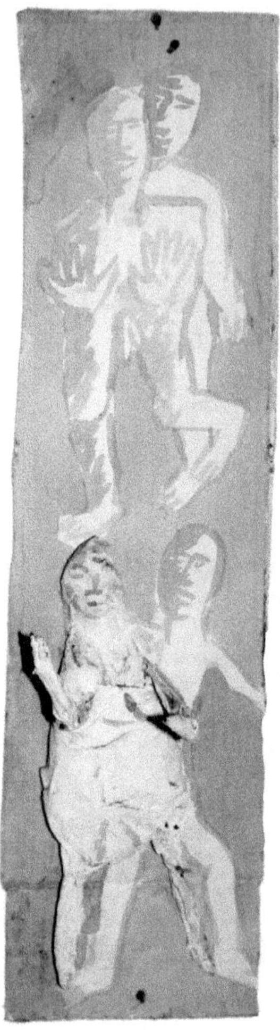

At Goddard I continued to do the bookkeeping but also was looking for shows to book, responding to mail, and things like that. As more and more puppeteers came, our family moved to other parts of the house that were not as spacious. Some of our children who wanted more of their own space built sleeping lofts or transformed spaces in the barn and out-buildings into their own rooms.

The Vietnam protests continued. I remember the train rides to the

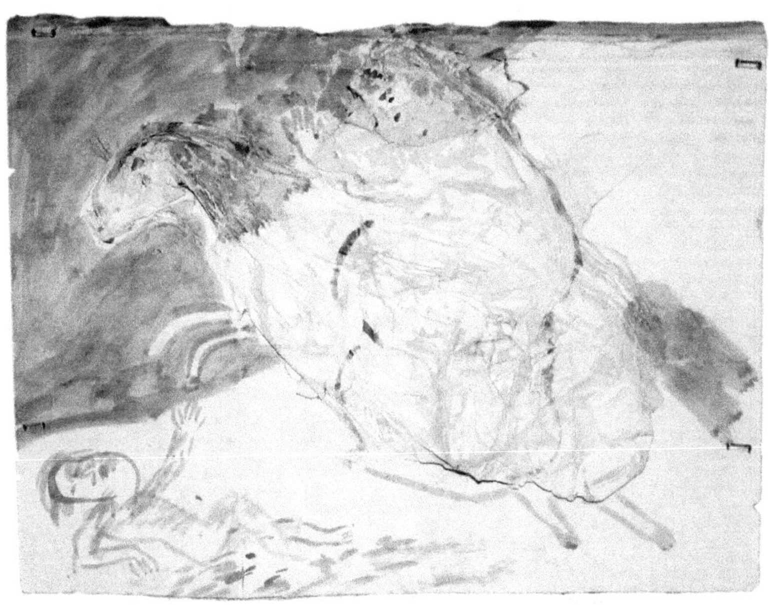

capitol in DC and being in these huge, huge demonstrations there with our puppets. But mostly I'd be observing and holding onto the kids.

MOVE TO GLOVER — After 4 years the college came to us and said—they were nice about it—but they said, "You are staying in temporary faculty housing and we have our next family that needs to be housed, so you have to find another place." At the same time my parents had bought the farm here in Glover. We didn't know they were looking

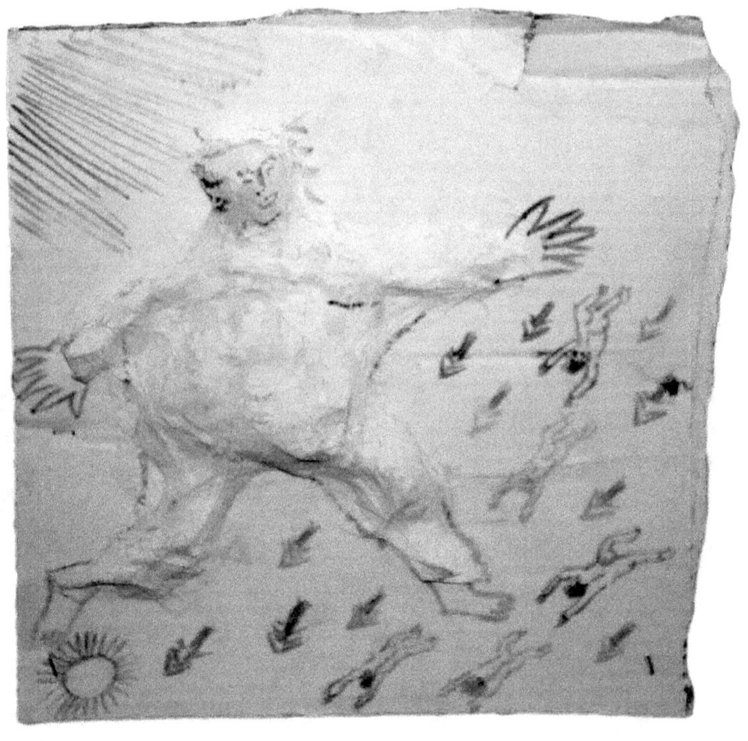

that hard for another place. They lived in suburban CT, and had decided, because they had paid off the mortgage, they would look for land in a more country area, and so they'd come to northern VT and gone to real estate people and been shown different places. When my mother first saw the Glover farm, the Bread & Puppet Farm, she saw it not from the road next to the farmhouse. The real estate person took them from the very back of the property, through a sugar bush, a beautiful wonderful forest,

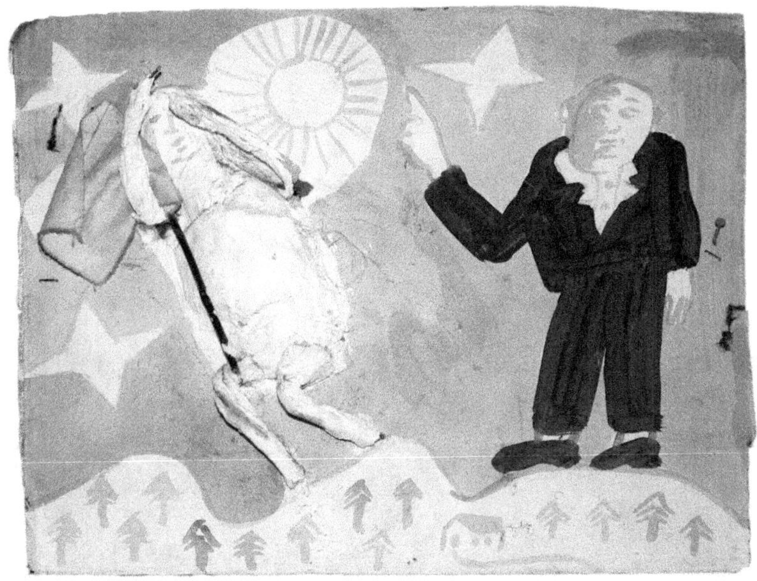

and then when you come out of the sugar bush you have a view over the whole farm to the circus field. And my mother, as a country woman, said this is the place that we want. So they bought the farm, but then very quickly decided it was too run down and they weren't that interested in renovating an old farm house and living so far away. It seemed like they'd made a mistake to buy it, but they saw how much we liked it. First some puppeteers came and stayed for the summer, and a couple of people

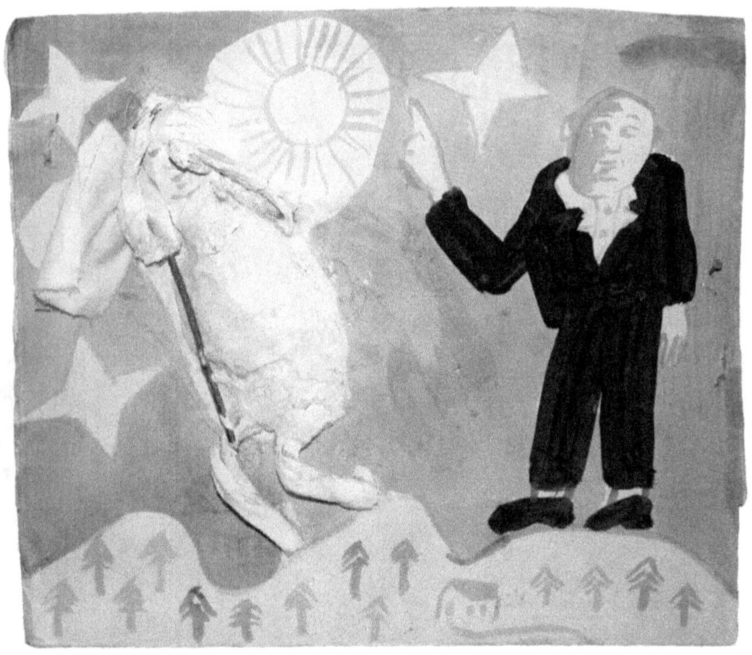

stayed for over a year, and by that time we had to get out of Cate Farm and so in the summer of 1974, we moved to the Glover farm with whoever wanted to stay in the company. That first winter we discovered how cold the totally uninsulated house could be! The Home Comfort kitchen cook stove that we still use today was our best heat source.

THE RESURRECTION CIRCUS — We had our first circus at Goddard in 1970, the summer after we moved to Vermont. Peter

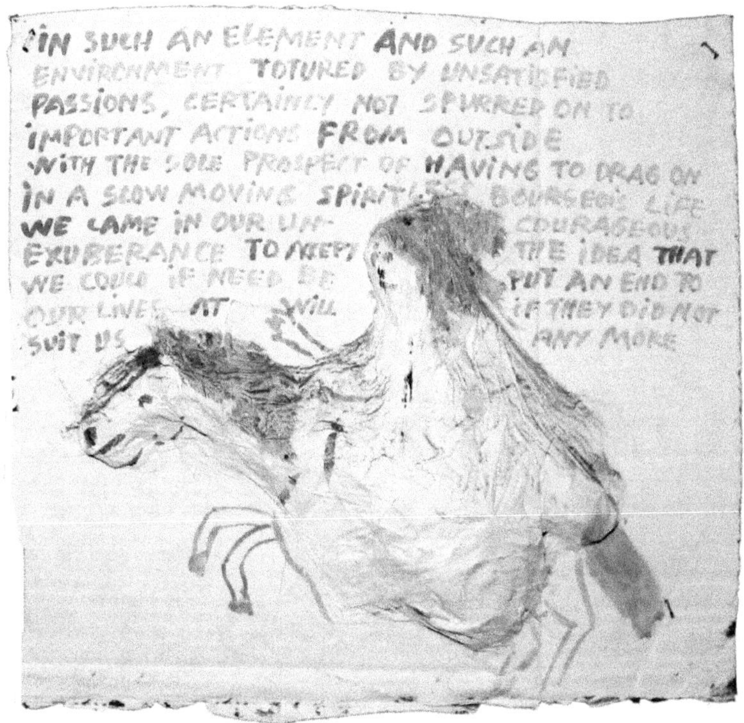

decided that the meadow needed a round show, and the most round show that we know is called the "Circus." We called it "Our Domestic Resurrection Circus" and we do it every summer. Instead of touring in the summer and making our living with tours, we decided to stay here, and enjoy life in the country and weather and the beauty of the surroundings, and work the whole summer towards this one big performance. And that's how we did it. It was always called "The 19th Annual"

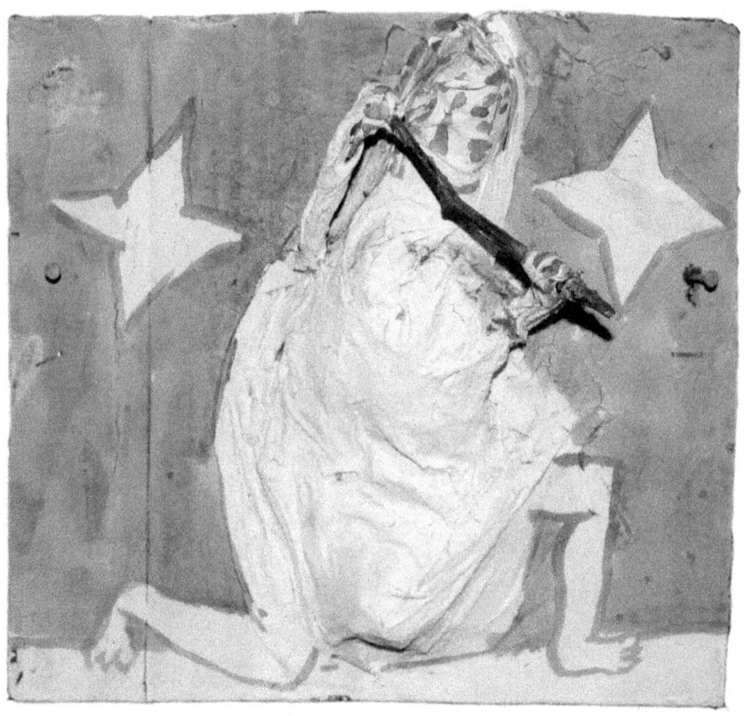

by Paul Zaloom, who made the big announcement at the beginning.

Peter had sort of disbanded the company when we moved to Glover, but some people—John Bell, Trudi Cohen, Michael Romanyshyn, Paul Zaloom—they stuck with it through thick and thin. It started small. We did the first two or three circuses on a small scale and the audience heard about it, and they came, and parked on the road on Route 122. They watched the shows and ate the bread and all that, and very quickly

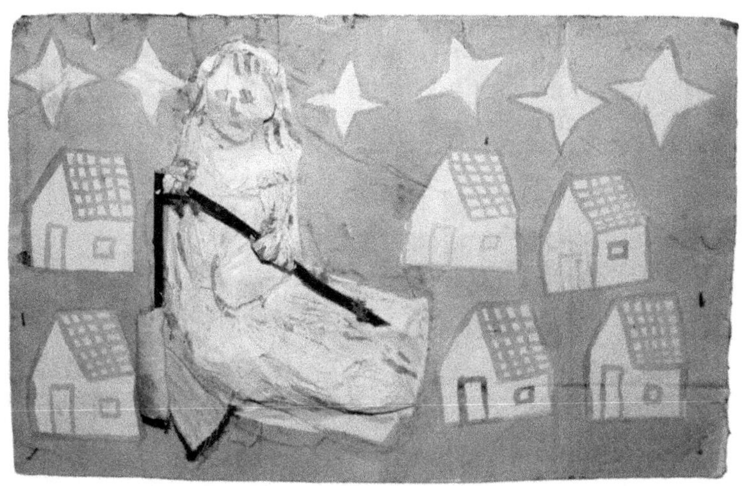

it started to grow, and very soon the town told us we could no longer use the road for parking. Our neighbors opened up their fields for parking, so more people could come. The word spread around about the event and we got on some kind of network. People who were coming to or from the Rainbow Gathering would stop at Bread & Puppet, and so we had bigger and bigger audiences. The local sheriff, Ray Young, who watched the parking and the audience, and took care of any emergencies that

SHE RIDES

came up, told us that the last performance drew about 30,000 people. There were many problems from having so many people. Peter had to bake bread for a couple of weeks before the show to make enough loaves to have for the performance. We had to build more outhouses, we had to bring more water up, we created an emergency station for sprained ankles and bee stings, and things like that.

Because of all these kinds of things preparation was intense. After

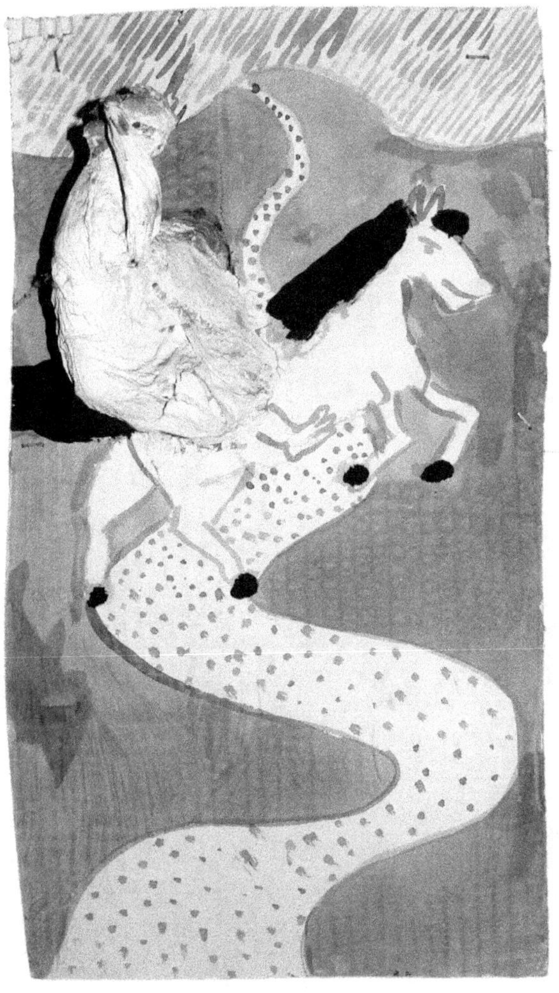

living down at the farmhouse from 1974 for six years and being in the very midst of the commotion and work and activity, especially in the summer preparing for the circus, I felt like it was too hard, it was too difficult. To live in the middle of it got to be really difficult, so that's when I wanted to say "no more circuses." I couldn't do that, but the solution seemed to be that we could have a house away from the center of all this activity. And we figured out an arrangement where we would get money

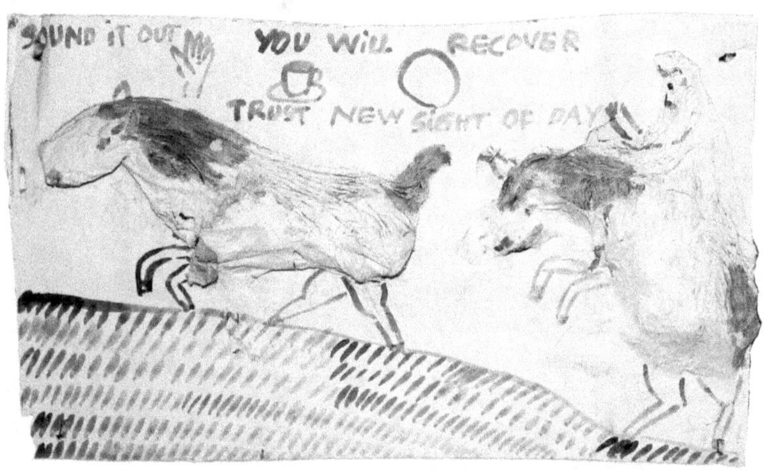

to build our own house in exchange for the puppeteers living out of the farmhouse. And that worked.

One of the attractions for us at the Glover farm was that in this huge 24-acre hayfield there was a gravel pit that made an amphitheater that worked beautifully for the circus. The gravel pit was dug to mix gravel for building Interstate 91, and for the first part of the time we were here, there were always dump trucks going back and forth, back and forth, carrying the gravel.

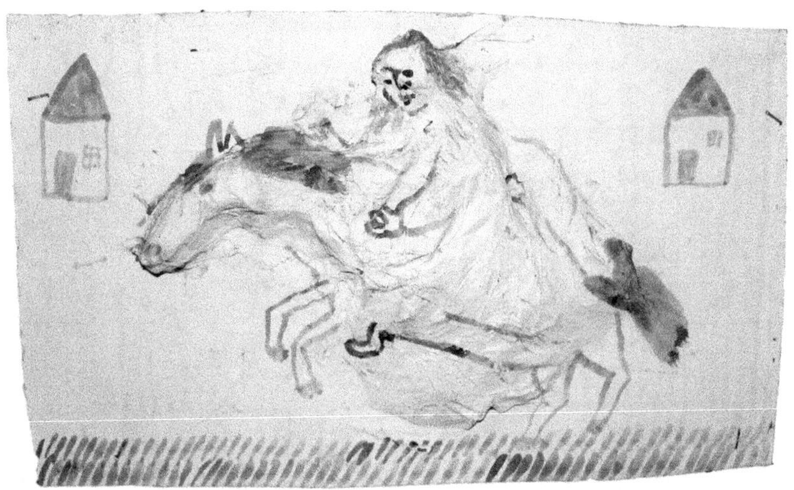

The circus would start things, with the band playing and one very big puppet opening it, and a lot of music, political acts and goofy acts. I played saxophone in the band; we played regular band tunes. The pageant would come afterwards, in the evening. The pageants were always part of it right from the beginning, even at Goddard. In Glover the audience would move up the hillside and have the bigger view of the whole area surrounding the fields.   On the rim of the circus field, when they

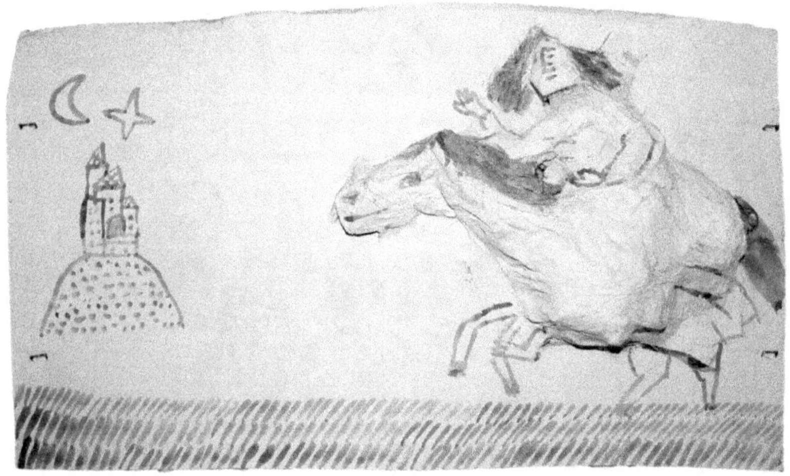

moved up the slope, they had the view of not just the amphitheater, but the meadow beyond. You could see the edge of the woods, the cupola of the barn, and with that view and all the people who were working with us you could really do grand, grand spectacles.

When we moved to Cate Farm, one of the first people we met was Larry Gordon who had discovered and fallen in love with Sacred Harp Music. It's Early American music, with notes written in four shapes, intended to

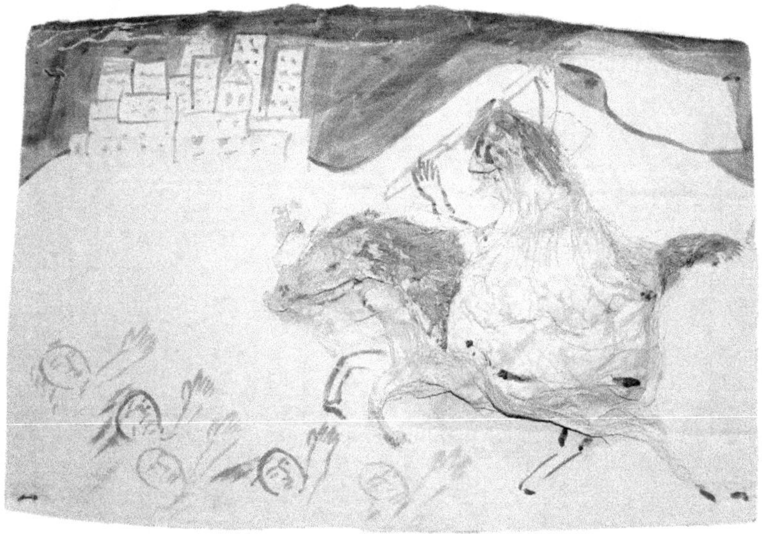

help everyone read music easily. The wonderful, sometimes discordant and primitive harmonies, are set to very, very pious biblical words. They're beautiful, and they certainly enrich the Bread & Puppet performances, even though they are not full of political ideas or anything like that. The music was attractive and easy to learn, and so we soon started meetings with singing a song together or having evenings just learning songs. We carried that tradition here to Glover and we still use the music, especially

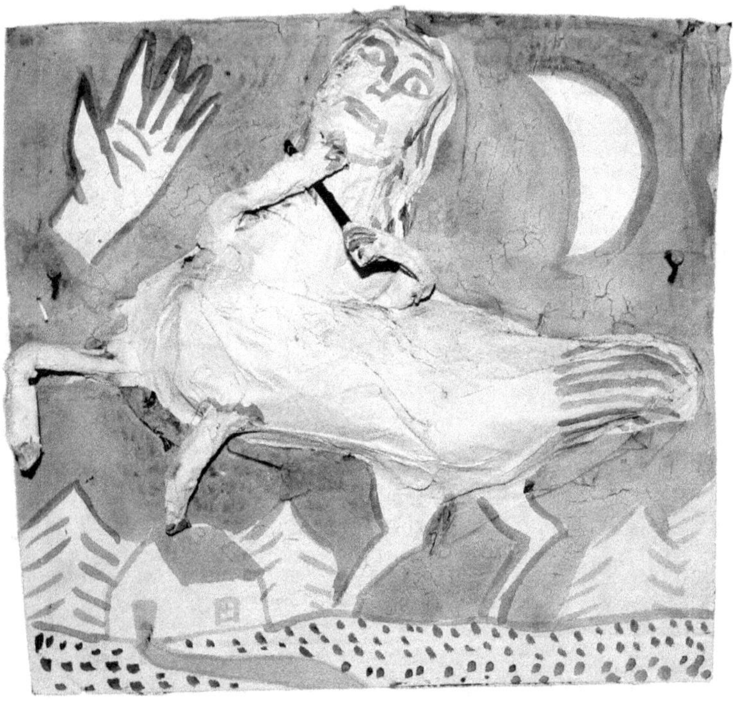

in the pageants. When the puppeteers tour, they learn the songs and sing in the bus so that everybody will be familiar with the same repertoire.

Peter started doing what he's doing a lot now, he's using cardboard paper maché. The puppets were made of paper maché, the big masks and the giant masks. Then when a hundred people were working on the circus, Peter said, "Let's invite the audience to be part of the circus, they can learn the songs that open the show, they can learn simple

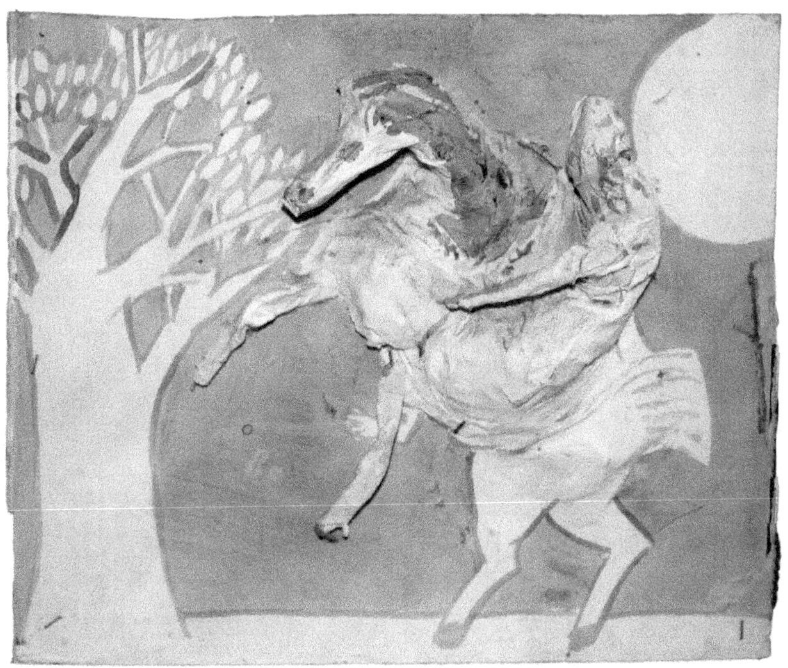

choreography, and instead of carrying or wearing puppets which would be hard and need more rehearsal, let them hold painted cardboard." One year it would be flowers, another year it would be sheaves of grain, another year figures, all just cut out of cardboard. That included more and more people all the time.

In terms of utilizing cardboard and other materials that would otherwise be thrown away, it just seemed so logical. You wouldn't go out to

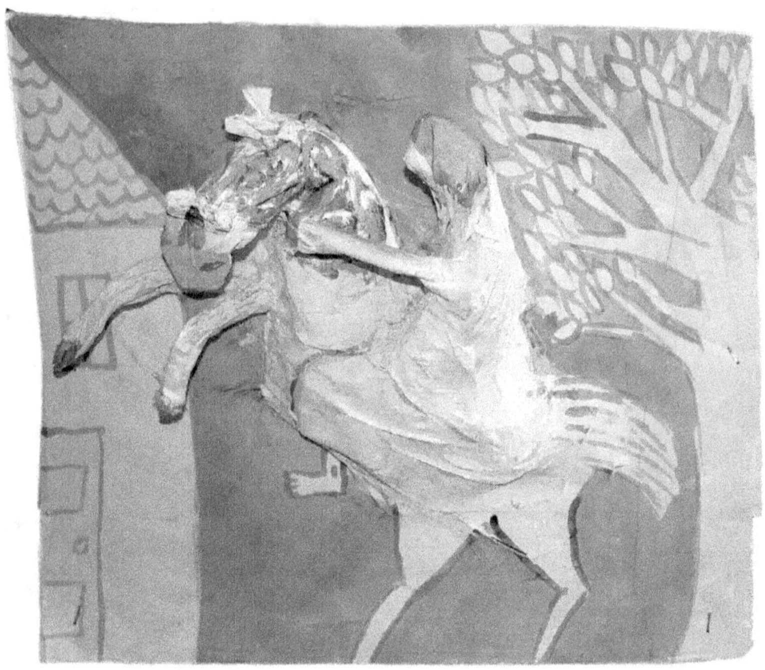

a store and buy some material or pipes if you needed to make vertical things, you'd go out in the woods and do some thinning in a poplar grove and there it is right there. You create maybe a little meadow by doing that. And the cardboard, everything comes in cardboard. Now it's worse because things come in plastic or foam or stuff like that. Cardboard you can reuse and it can last for quite a while, but with the plastic wrapping, even tiny little things are bound up in layers of it.

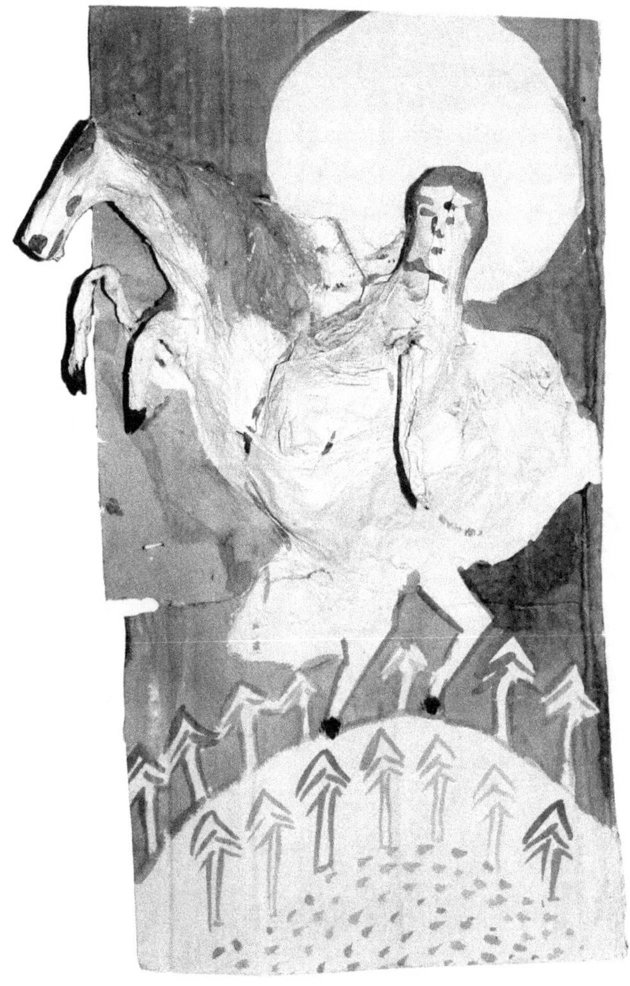

THE PRESS — The company was occupied with getting a show ready, rehearsing, and touring. My kids were getting bigger and didn't need all the care, and I helped a lot with the theater because I was more available. But still, taking care of the family was a main concern, so working at printing was something I could do on my own time and fit into my schedule. We started selling the print art work on tours. We thought we should have a more organized printing project here, and who wants to do

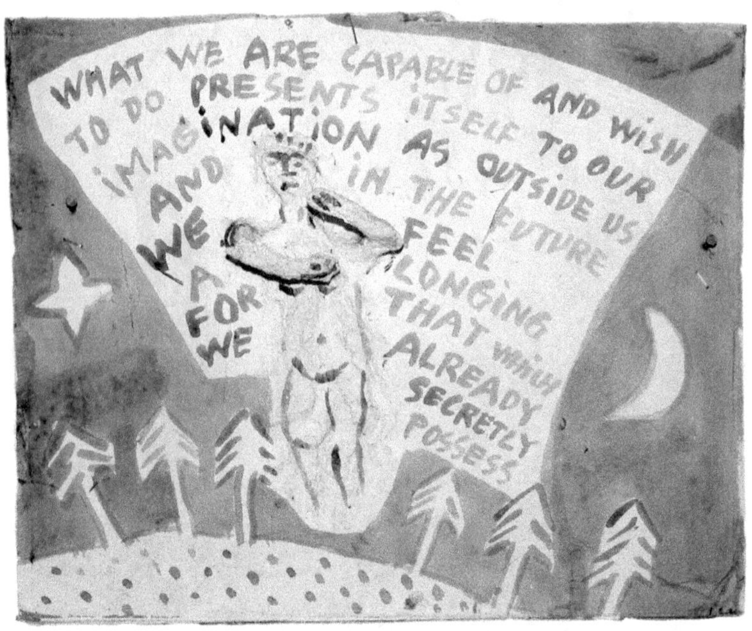

it? The puppeteers would reluctantly raise their hand, "Okay, I will," but they'd never have the time to get to it and so somebody at the next meeting would offer reluctantly to do it. It just became clear that they didn't have the time, so I said I would do it. I remember having a discussion about what should we call this thing—I was trying to think of a poetic name or something extraordinary, but someone said, "Let's just call it the Bread & Puppet Press," so that was easily solved. On the farm there's

SHE
FLIES

a room that had once been a ballroom back when the farm was a stage-coach stop, and that was the printing place for many years. We'd have to clear it out for meetings or for rehearsals in winter. Someone built very nice racks that could be pulled up to the ceiling, and we could hang the drying posters and banners on the racks and haul them up to the ceiling. Then we decided to have a store in the museum. We put up counters and tables and started doing a real production there. On tours the products

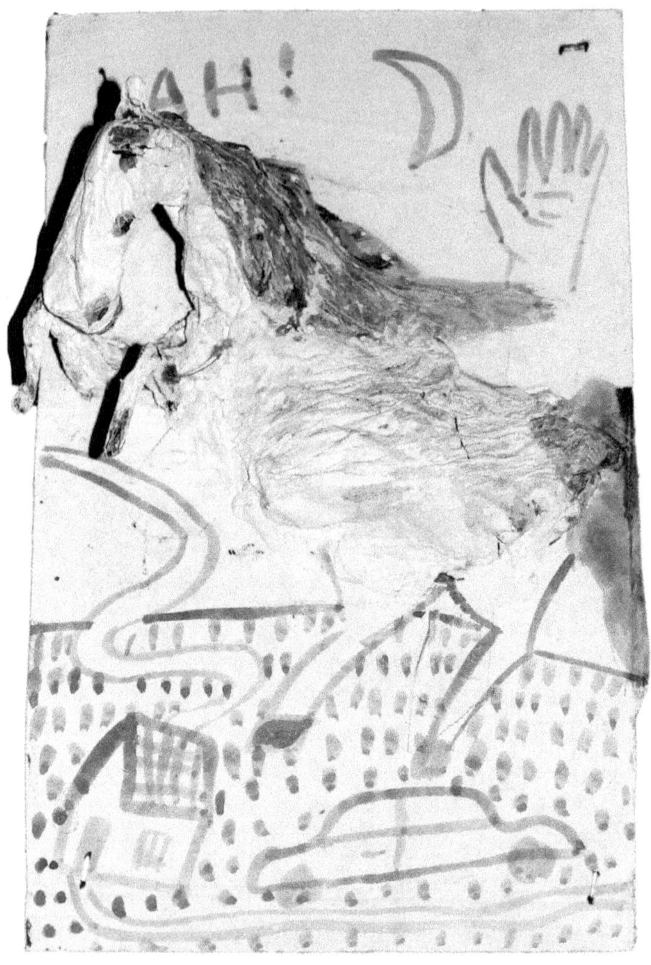

got sold and then sometimes we'd go to fairs and have sales tables there. For decades Lila Winstead was the main printer and very much involved in the whole activity of the store and the printing projects. And Peter just keeps making more and more cuts.

We decided not to sell T shirts. I feel like when our children, or our grandchildren, are starving then we'll sell T shirts. It seems like such a cheap, cheap thing to do, and if people want to buy a banner and some

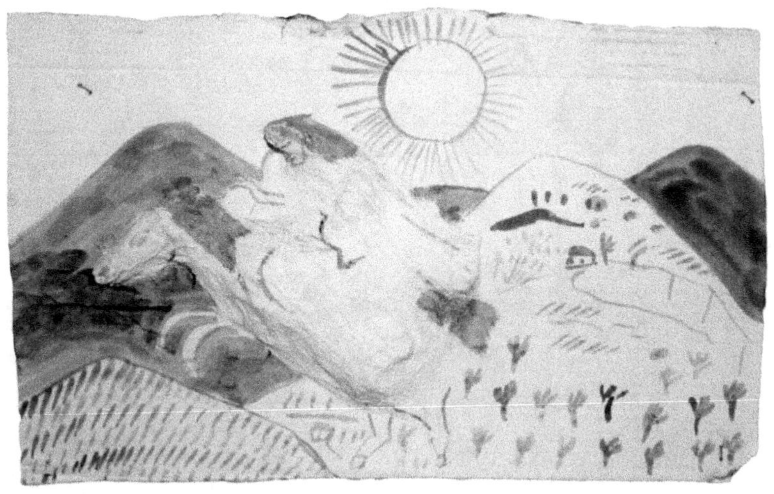

of the other prints, and sew it on their shirt or whatever, that's their business, but for the theater to do it, no. If we put Coca Cola signs on the banners we could make more money, but we don't.

Our posters are something that someone can take home and put on their wall, and show their friends, and if people like the art they could find out more about the theater, about our activity, our political activities, and participation in demonstrations and so on. A lot of Peter's graphics

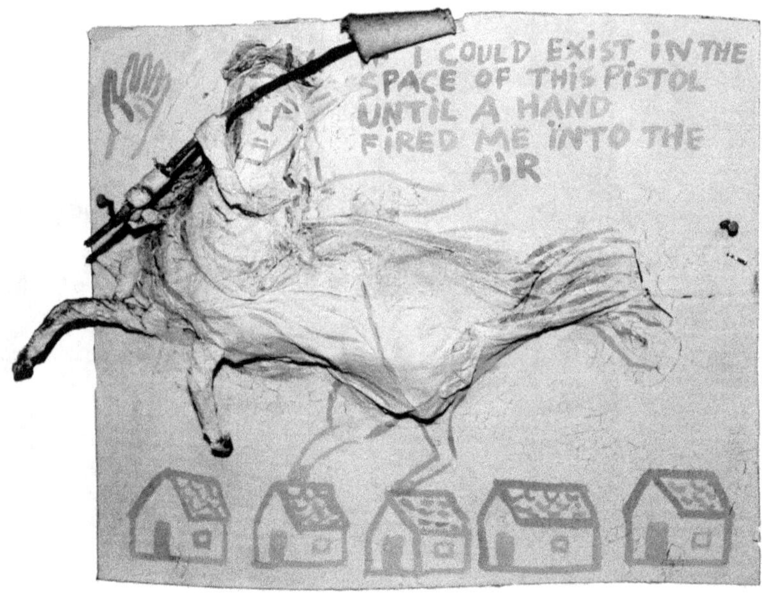

are very loose and fluid, but the wood cuts have a kind of solidity about them. They're not always trying to give a particular message. We have our poppies with RESIST above them, or the rooster and RISE UP, and people can make their own connections to those things.

The sale of our graphics, booklets, and books, and our best sellers, the posters and the postcards, is quite considerable, it's between 80 and 100 thousand dollars a year. Peter makes little books and now he's found

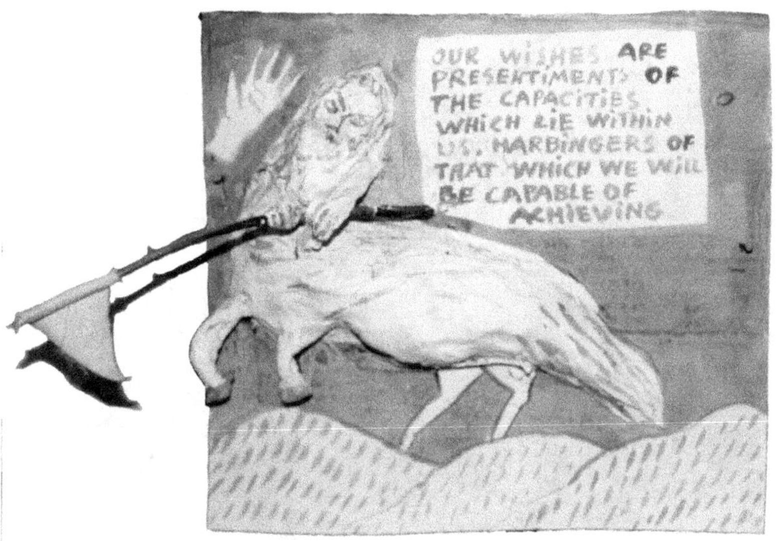

a way to make books with spines. They are very reasonably priced, but people aren't reading or buying books as much; they want something to put on the wall. The money made from the press is a good contribution to the theater. We used to keep the press income separate from the theater income, and then transfer chunks of it into the theater. We try to cover all of our material expenses: the fabric, paint, and inks, and salaries for some of the helpers. Most of the press workers have been from the

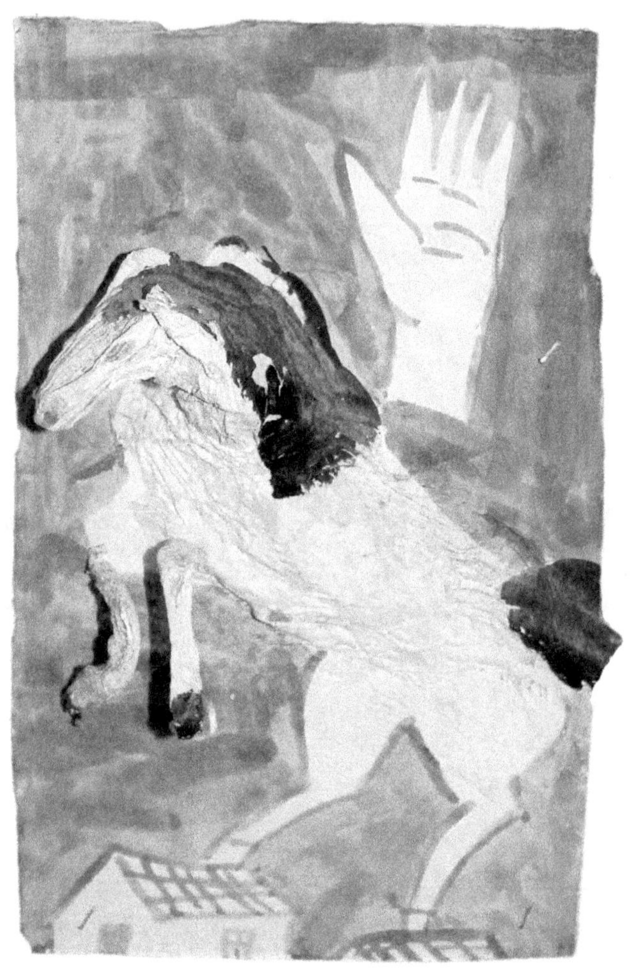

company; they participate by working in the press, and it brings money in for everything.

ORGANIZATIONAL EVOLUTION OF THE THEATER AND PRESS —The theater also has become much more organized, with people more seriously in charge of certain aspects of it. There's more specialization, so now some of the company are gardeners, some are cooks, some take charge of the workshop to provide better overview of things.

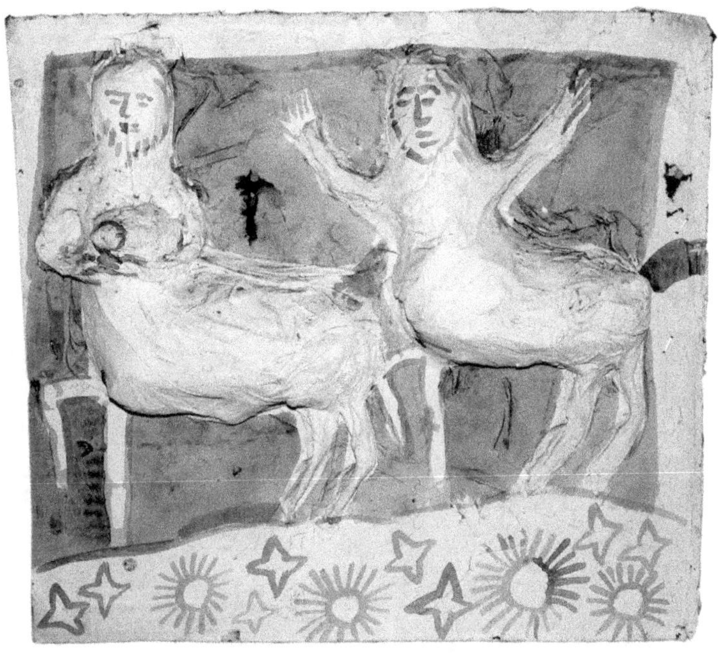

In the old days it was looser, and things got confused, though mostly, things worked out well. Now there's a finance committee and budgets are made, and things continue to work out well.

More people are involved more seriously now and they want to feel more secure, and have better direction or know what's expected of them. On the whole it's working well, so we're not complaining about it, but it is different.

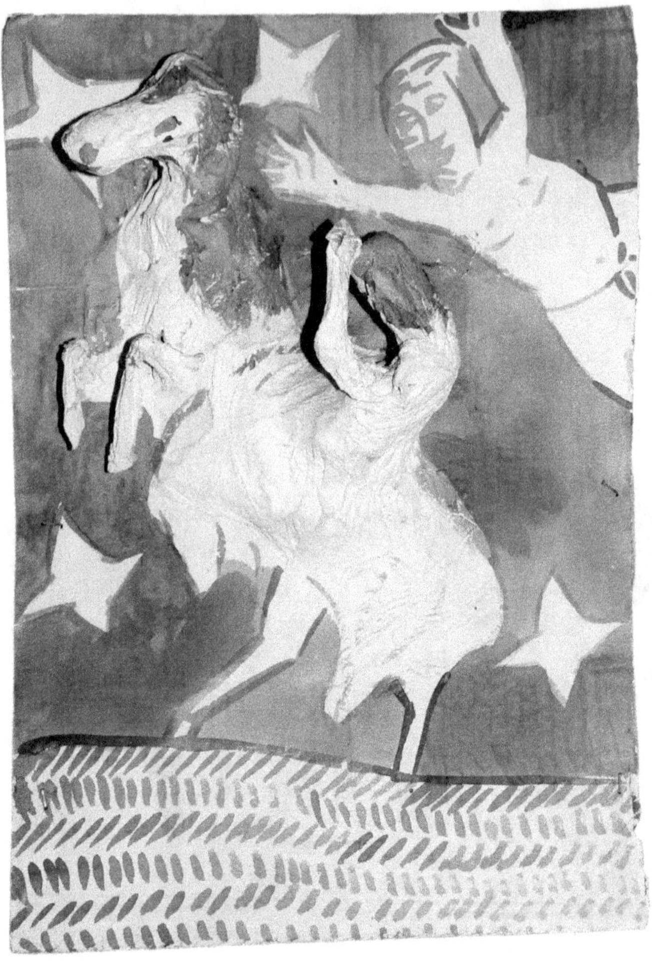

Now we have electronic media getting the message out about the Theater. Before we would do mailings and send out brochures. Now whoever would like to hear more about Bread & Puppet can find it on the internet.

We've traveled a lot and made international connections, so many people know about us. In the early summers here in Glover there was a wonderful teacher at the University of Puerto Rico, who told her students

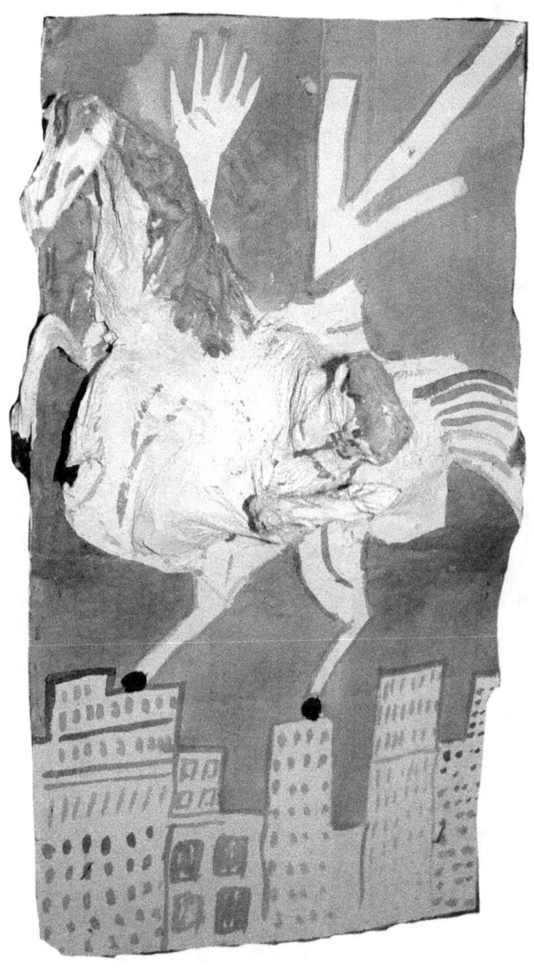

about Bread & Puppet and for several summers these great kids came up. They were so hard-working and friendly and excited and talented. We developed strong Puerto Rican connections. And people from other countries, like Greece, and from Germany, and France come and we encouraged them teach us their songs and we work together.

THE NAME BREAD & PUPPET/OTHER THOUGHTS — The name Bread & Puppet? I've been giving museum tours for a bunch of

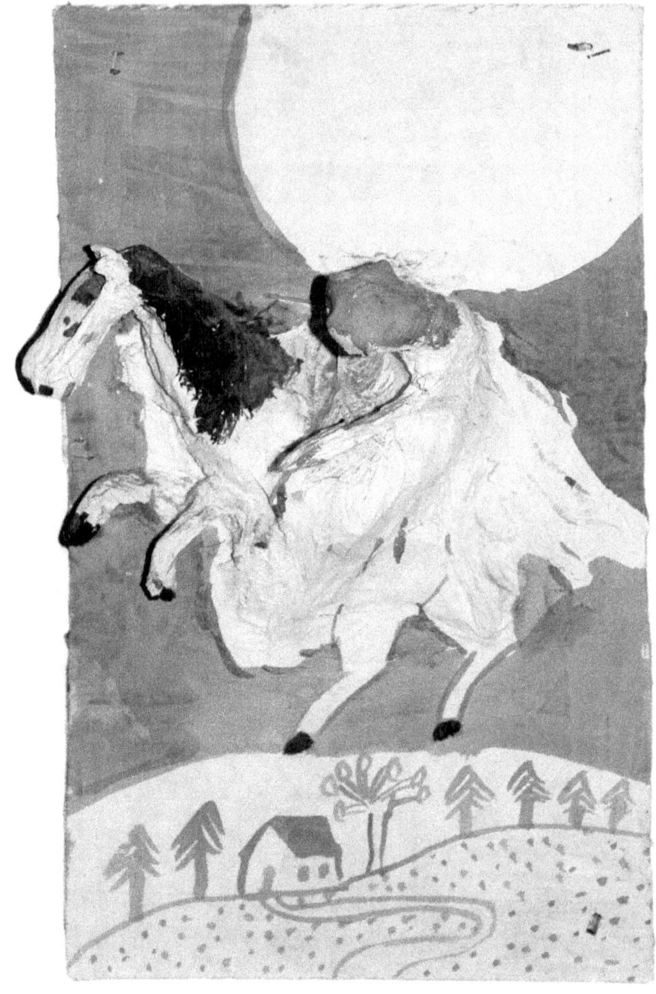

years, and I start by the bread oven, which is at the entrance way into the museum. There's a sign that says Bread & Puppet, and I just say: Bread is the first word in our name and it is a really big and important component of the whole, the work here and the life and art. Peter learned to bake from his mother. It's just part of the essence of life. It seems so obvious.

For me, it's very moving when people that you don't know at all come up at the Bread House or at some performance and say, "Oh, I

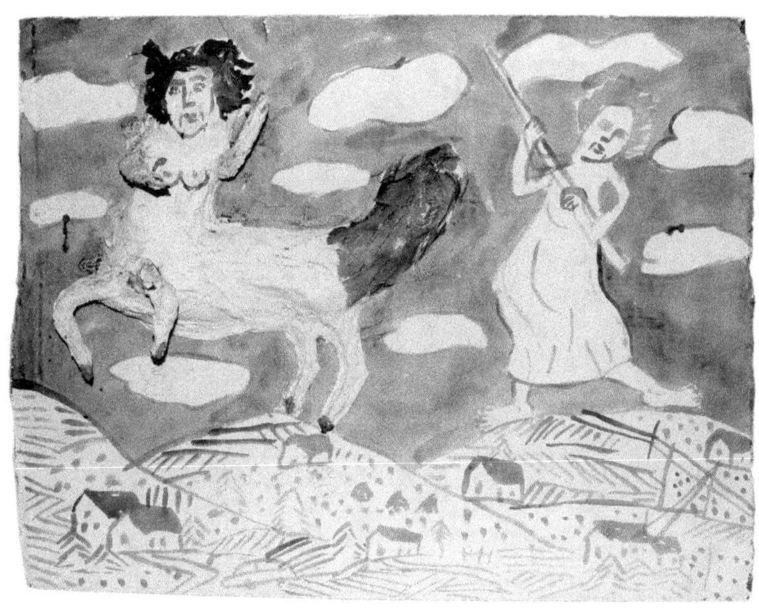

saw you when I was a little child, it was so wonderful to come here."

About the concept of "possibilitarianism," the book on which that phrase is based is Robert Musil's *The Man Without Qualities*. It's called in German *Der Mann ohne Eigenschaften*. And it's just saying anything is possible, and it's so open and in a way hopeful. It's nice to have an idea like that now.

But we should never forget that when anyone makes grand statements about Bread & Puppet, that not everyone knows what it means. For some,

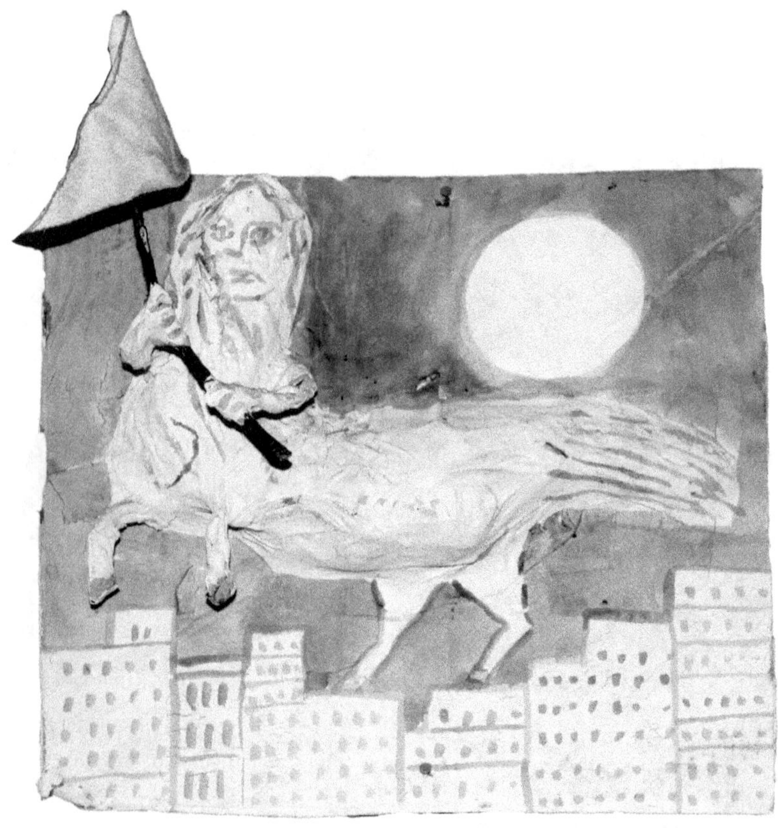

Bread & Puppet is recognizable and evokes impressions and memories, but for a huge majority of the world, it's absolutely unknown and meaningless. Just a couple of years ago there were interns who talked about that: "Oh I had these certain ideas, but I was in a bubble, and didn't reach out and had no contact with others. But here, I feel so like my peers, with my fellow believers." I think that in a way Bread & Puppet is a bubble, but it's a bigger bubble. If it could reach everywhere, the world wouldn't be…so divided.

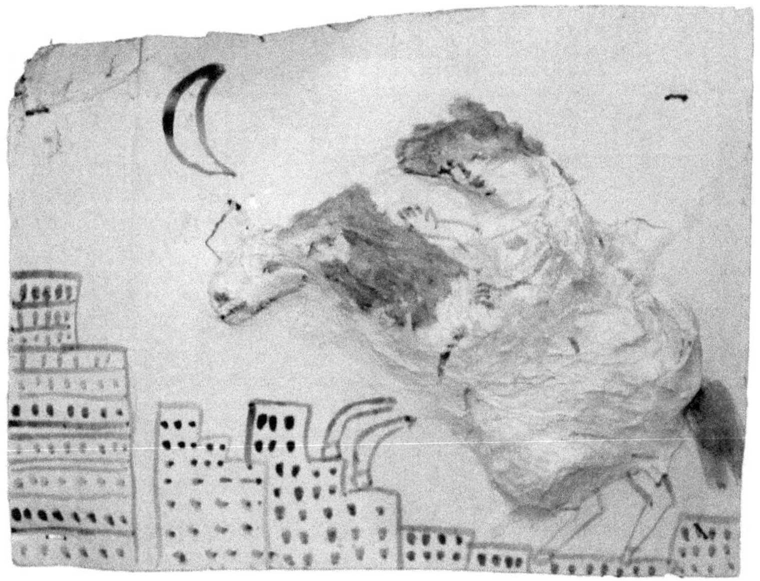

THE MUSEUM — The museum has become one of the great attractions of this place. It's such a beautiful stately building. Upstairs, it was full of old hay, it wasn't even real hay, it was chaff which is broken up bits of hay, and it was knee high or deeper. The side aisles also were full of hay, and there was old equipment there—old sleds and stone sleds and grinding machines for corn and so on. When we came, we spent the first months just cleaning out all that debris. The chaff was very hard to move because you

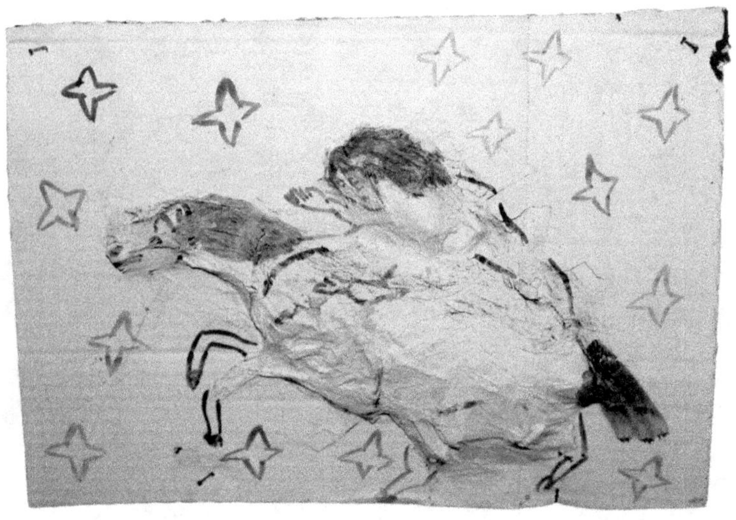

couldn't push a shovel into it, it was too dense, and if you used a pitch fork the chaff just trickled through the tines. It required a big, intensive cleaning. There's also an attic in the barn where more hay was stored. All of that had to get tumbled down and thrown out, or swept out through the double doors. We started a big haystack at the foot of the double doors. There was a high-drive ramp there and the horses used to pull up the wagon full of hay into the main aisle of the barn. At first the haystack was really big, but

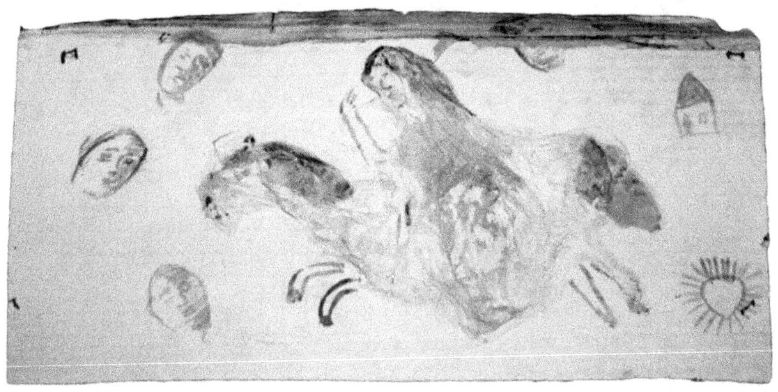

it quickly just rotted into a wonderful fertilizer for the garden.

We needed places for the puppets that we had brought here from Cate Farm. We worked upstairs first because the big puppets were the ones we wanted to display, so as soon as we got an area cleared we mounted the big puppets there. A lot of them are still where they were first put, but many more have been added over the years, and more have been stuck on the ceiling, on the walls, and paintings, and banners hung from the

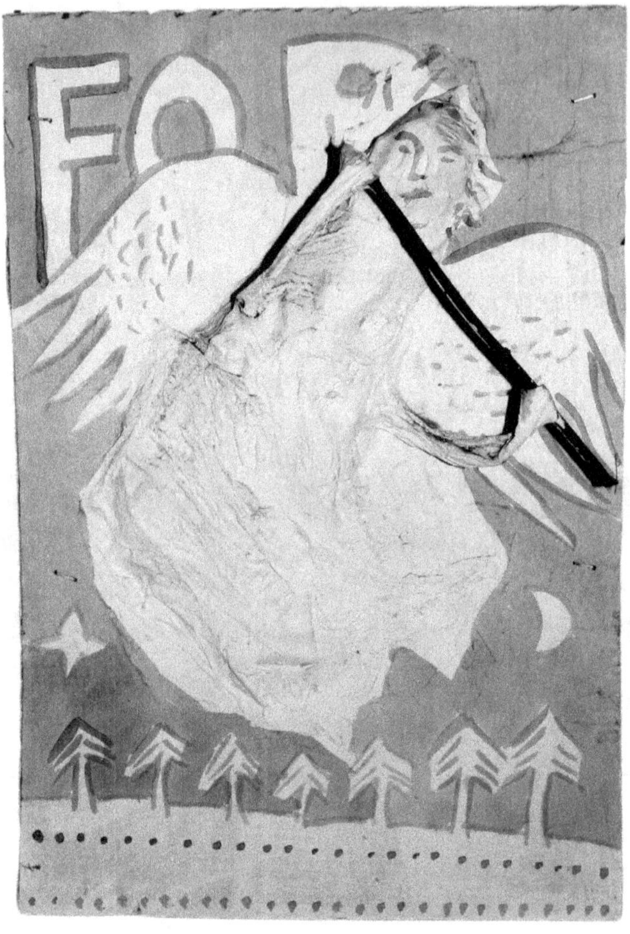

beams. First, we stored our empty boxes downstairs and then said why not make that a museum too. So that's how that started. I don't know how long I have been doing the museum tours — at least a couple of decades. The tours feel like a good way to introduce people to the history of Bread & Puppet and some of the ideas that are here.

CHEAP ART — Peter came up with the idea, "Cheap Art." It came after there was a run of ads in the New York Times by ExxonMobil

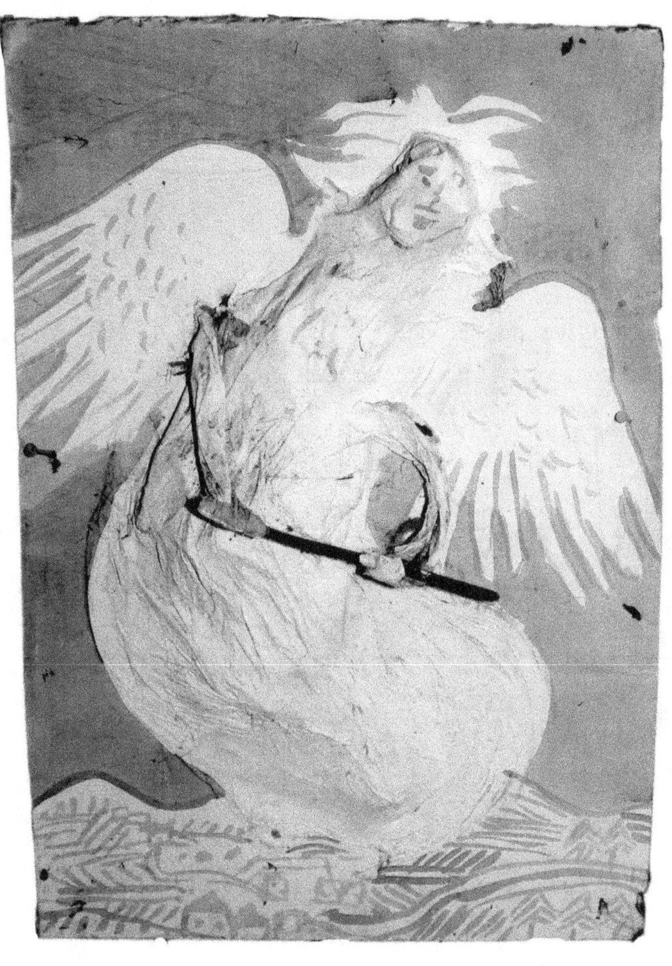

supporting fancy art projects, and Peter said, "No, art should be cheaper, it should be for the people." He wrote some manifestos and some flyers with strong words about what art is good for, and our son Max took this idea. Max was a great painter and did a lot of his own cheap art. He made pictures of cars and used magazine covers as background. Then we started a cheap art store in the school bus across the street from the farmhouse. Originally, prices were indeed like between 15 cents and 3 dollars. Now

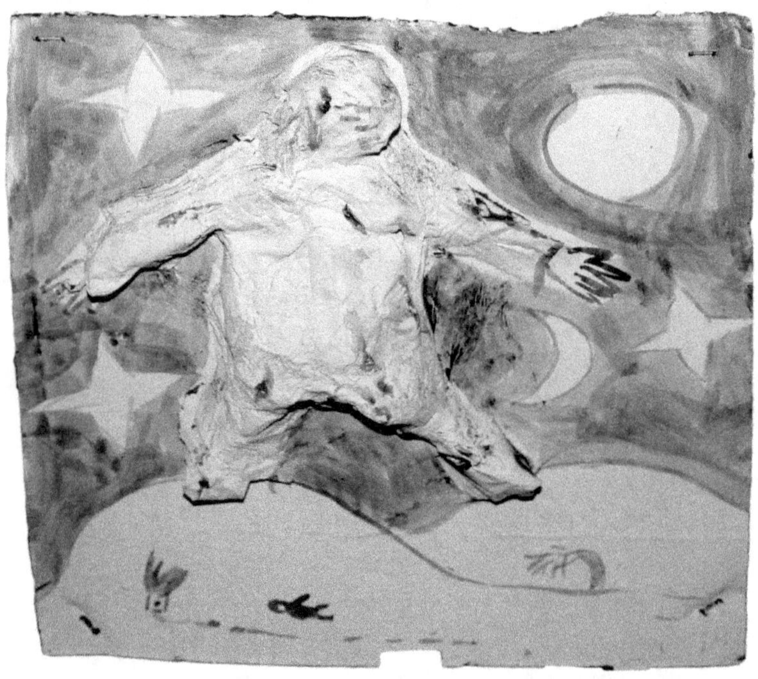

the artists are getting more ambitious and asking for higher prices, but still, compared to commercial art, anyone who likes a painting or a print can have one for affordable prices.

IMPERMANENCE/MEMORIAL FOREST — There is a nice little thing that Peter wrote that's on the cover of our museum brochure. He talks about the art of impermanence. We know that fire is a huge hazard. Anybody smoking or whatever could start that. The other

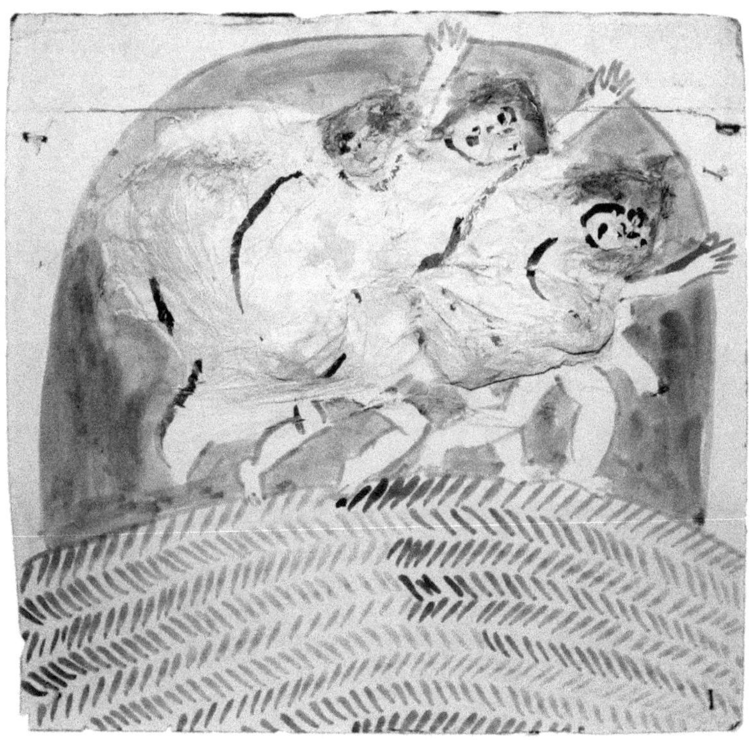

hazard is the little bugs, powder post beetles, that live in the wood. These old dry beams and boards are 180-years old. The bugs chew up the wood and create this fine dust and wherever they been at work you see a little tiny pile of yellow dust. When we do the cleanup in the spring these piles are all over the place, so they have been at work all winter. We've asked about how to treat it and they say borax, you paint the place with borax, or you could wrap it up in plastic and pump some

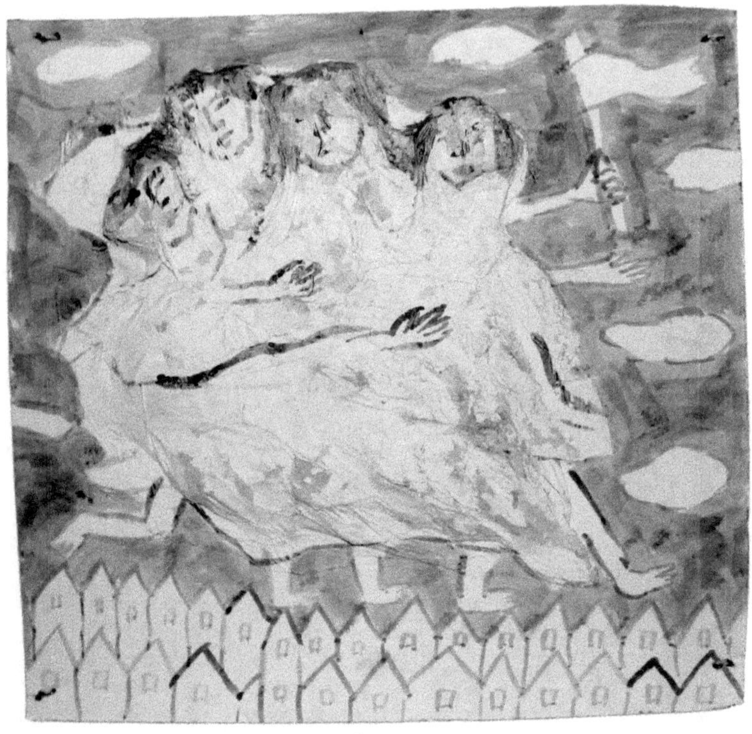

bad gases into it, but we haven't done any of that. So we know it isn't going to last, nor are we.

It's different now because we're in our eighties. Peter really wants to do the theater, he wants to build things, to make paintings, and create shows of different sizes and all, so he's doing that; that's happening. For me, it's been hard sometimes just because of daily tasks. I have more time now, but less ability to go out and do things. Now my place of interest

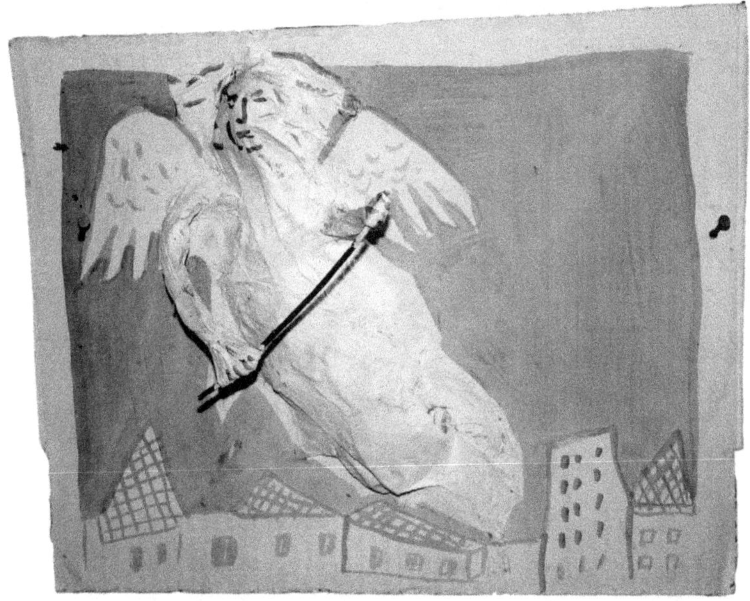

and activity is in the music in the summer, and in the print shop. It's worked out, but it hasn't always been easy.

When we moved here, we did a big show in a pine forest, based on, I think, a Bach Cantata. It was a wonderful place to perform. There is a nice gentle slope into the pine forest from the edge of the circus field above, so over the years we made a couple of places where performances could be given. I don't remember how it started being a memorial place,

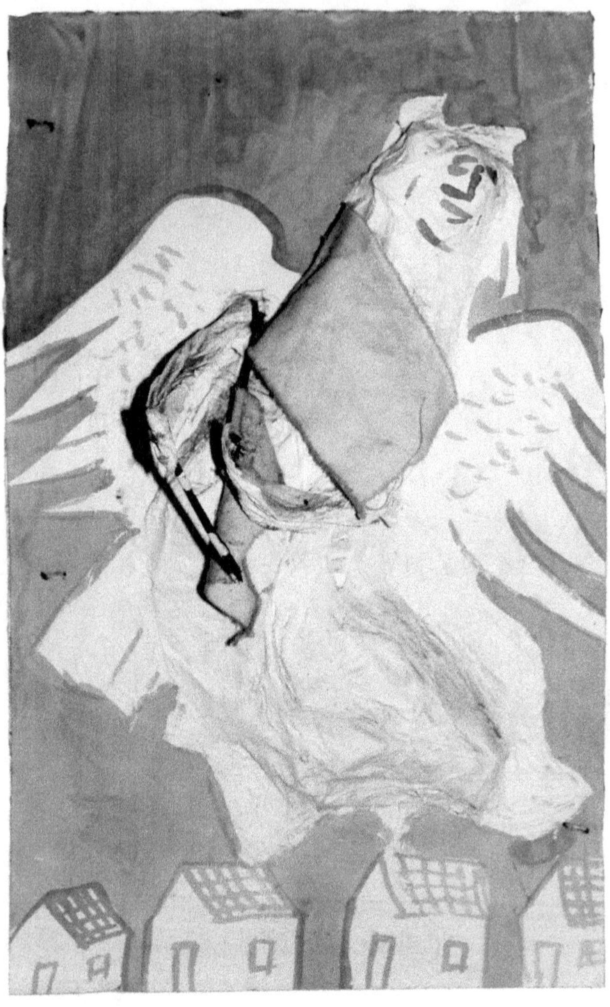

but that's been quite a while. Friends of ours who died, beginning in the seventies and through today, are memorialized there. It seems like a very beautiful place to go to and think of them and remember them.

Just a few years ago Peter had an idea to start a weekly walk there. Before that, when there was a death of somebody we knew and loved, we would have a real service for them, with a gathering at the farm house

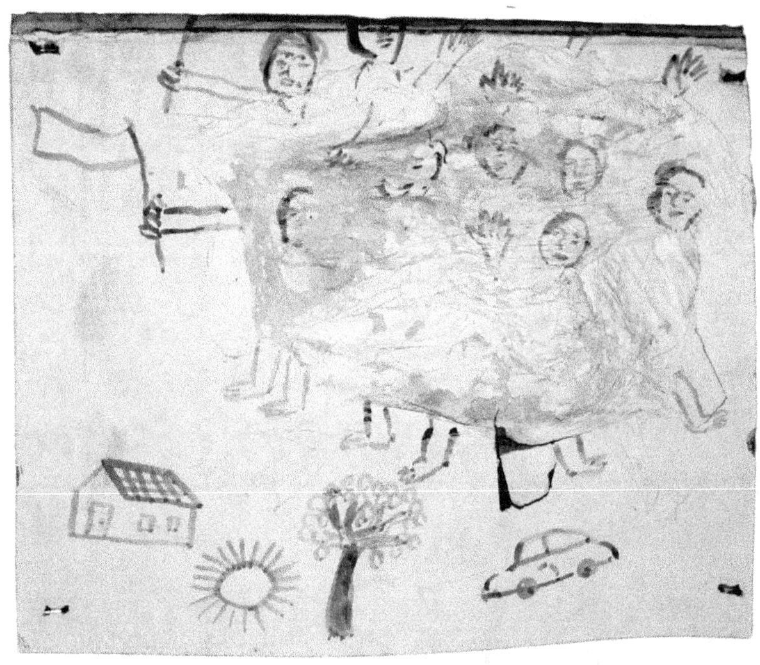

and a parade over the field with a band ending up in the pine forest, and we would remember the person and share memories. Then we started this other way of just gathering there without any big announcements or any specific event, to make it a regular part of the week. It's been very nice to come there. People speak up, as the spirit moves them. There are a couple of persons' ashes there, but mostly it's just a commemoration.

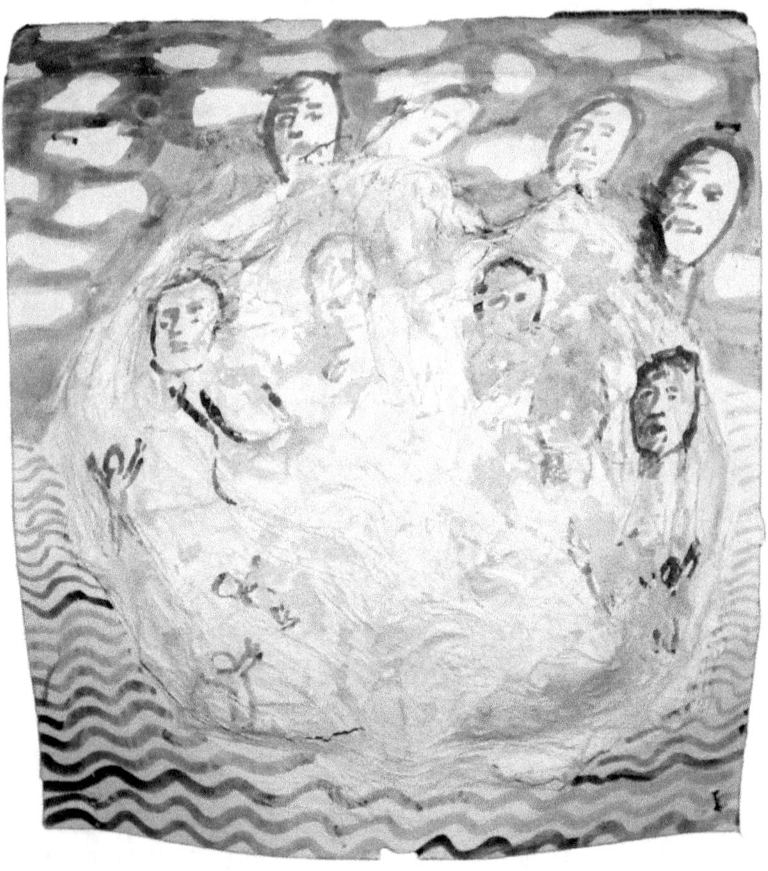

I think I'd rather be in a regular cemetery, but Peter wants to be in the
Pine Forest. It is something we need to talk about.

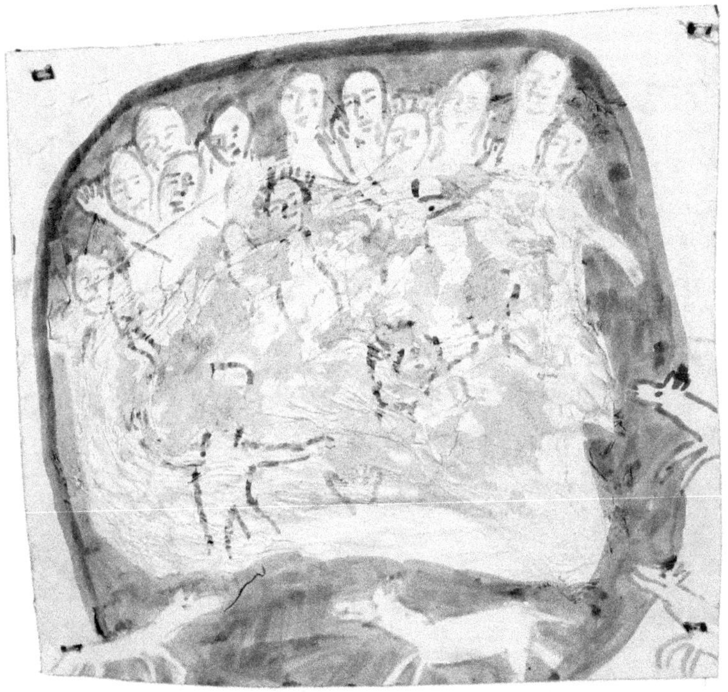

Peter — "In the end we agreed on a conjugal grave in the pine forest on the Bread and Puppet farm to honor the many puppeteers and relatives who are memorialized there."

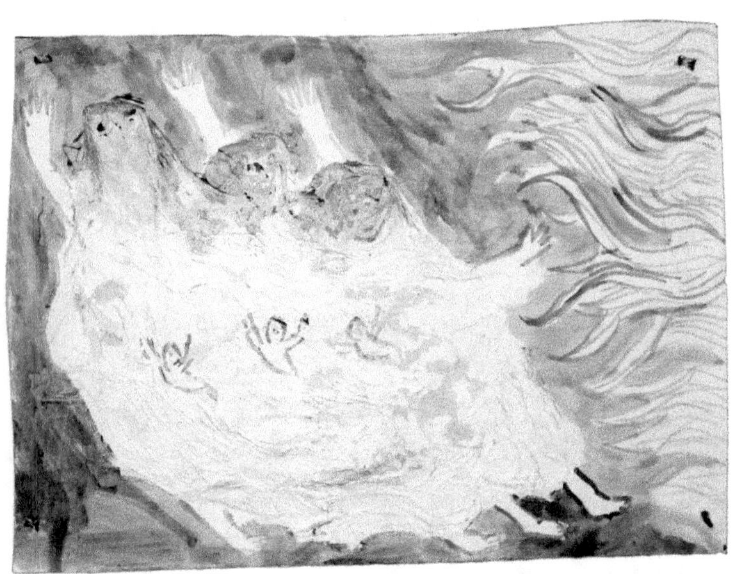

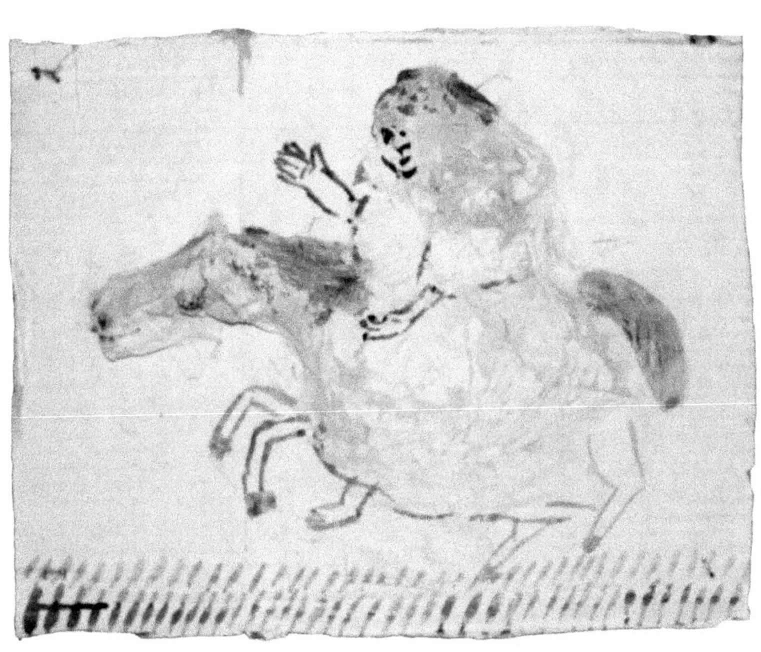

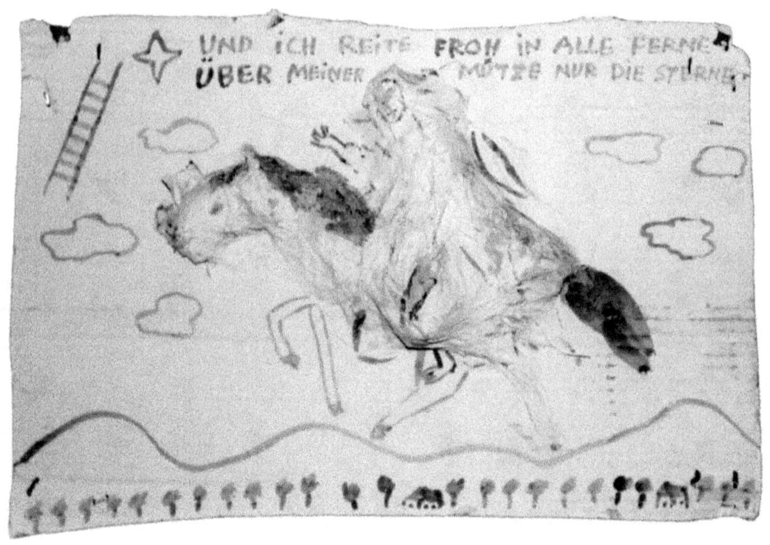

UND ICH REITE FROH IN ALLE FERNE
ÜBER MEINER MÜTZE NUR DIE STERNE

Und ich reite froh in alle Ferne,
Über meiner Mütze nur die Sterne.

And I ride happily into the distance,
Only the stars over my head.

—Goethe, "*Freisinn*/Free Spirit")

About this book

These bas-relief scenes, some with sculpted figures, were made by Peter Schuman in the early 1970s, and hung below waist-height along the low partitions separating the museum floor from the exhibit space. With huge figures, and myriads of masks displayed beyond them, the bas-reliefs are scarcely noticed by visitors, indeed are often swept over by pant legs and winter coats, destroying some of the flags the figures were holding, and wearing away at their painted surfaces.

Donna photographed them in situ, and, in making this book fifty years after their creation, I attempted to piece together a story they collectively tell. Elka Schumann's death (August 2021) prompted us to include a biographical narrative pieced together from several interviews with Elka, in parallel with Peter's earlier images, each telling its own analogous story.

Marc Estrin
Donna Bister
Fomite Press

About the text

The bulk of Elka's narrative was transcribed by Robin Lloyd from interviews conducted for *Bread and Puppet: Theater of the Possibilitarians* (working title), a forthcoming film directed by Robbie Leppzer, with Robin Lloyd, executive producer (www.BreadandPuppetMovie.com). The transcriptions were further edited by Elka. To that text Marc Estrin added elements of earlier interviews with Elka done by her daughter, Maria Schumann, for the Vermont Folkife Center and StoryCorps. After her first stroke, Elka worked with her friend and neighbor, Joanie Alexander, to edit a final text, an experience that sustained and delighted her during her healing. After her death from a second stroke, the "Elka-Joanie version" was proofread and additionally edited by Peter Schumann, Tamar Schumann and Josh Krugman, puppeteer.

Fomite books by Peter Schumann

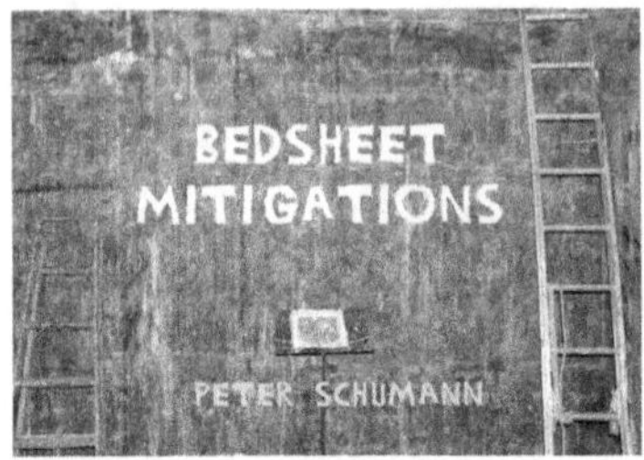

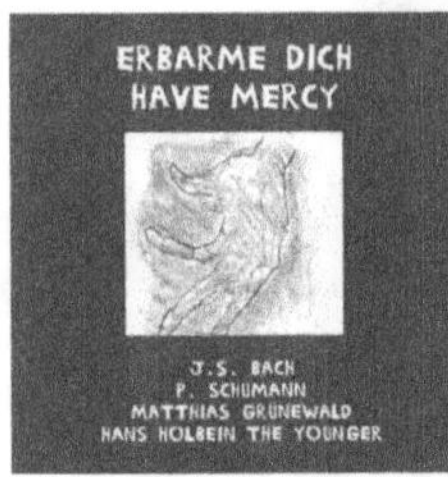

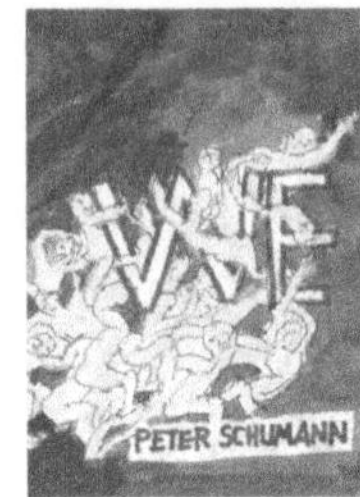

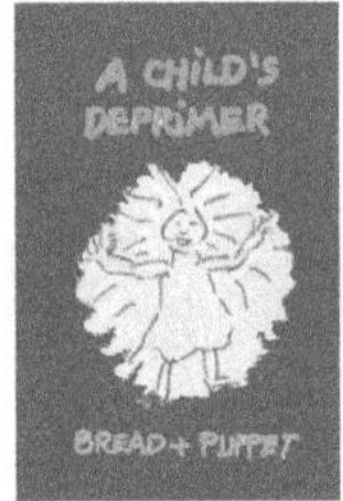

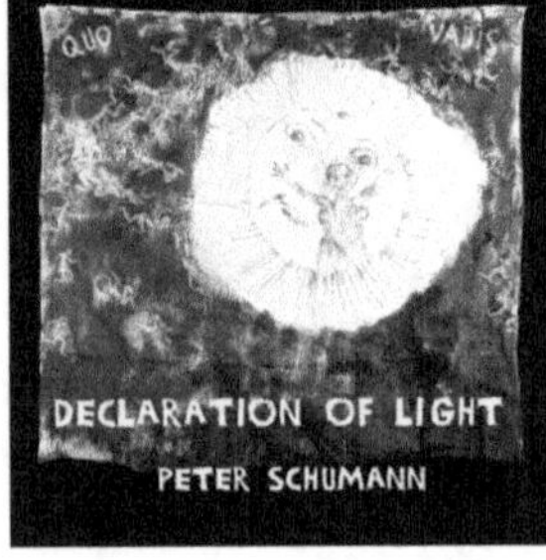

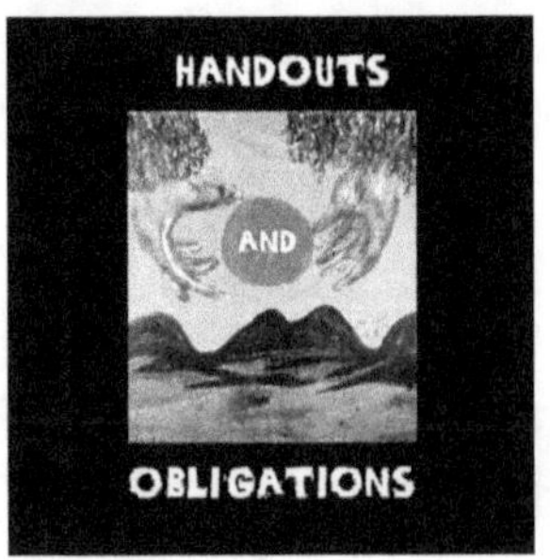

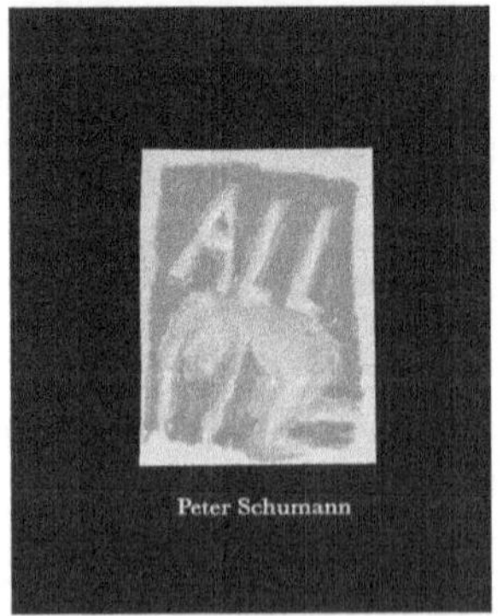

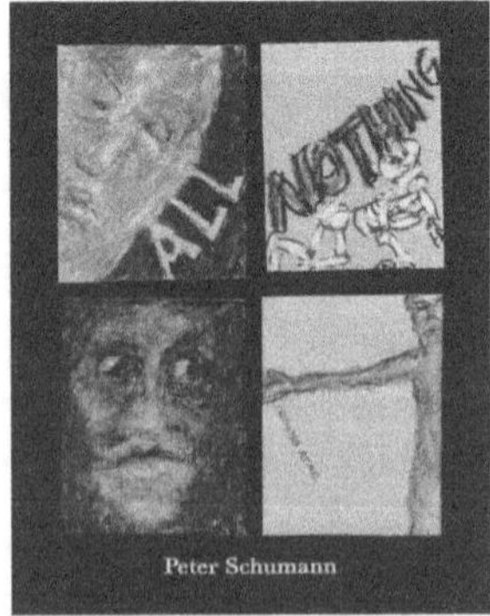

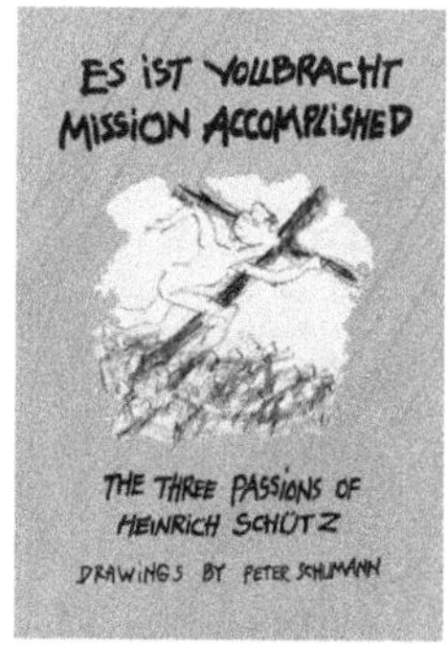

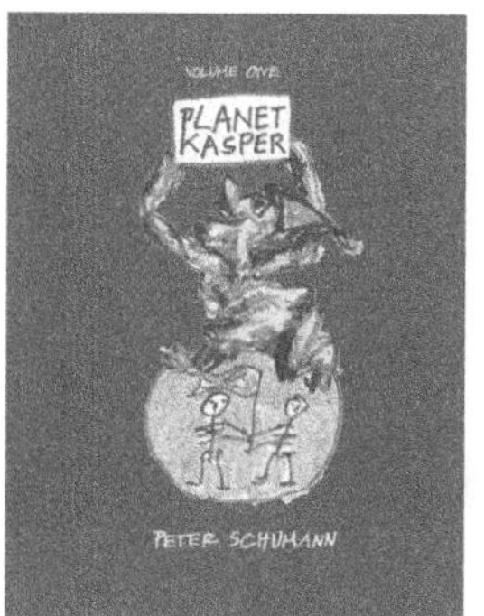

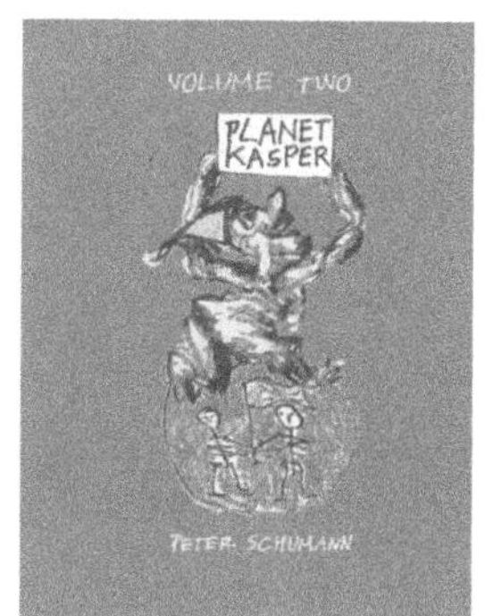

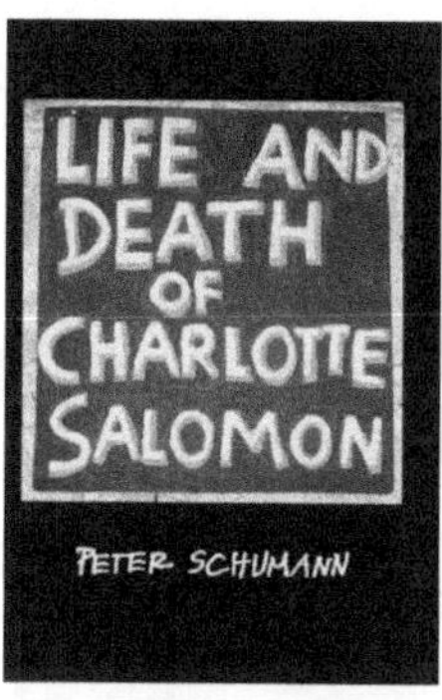

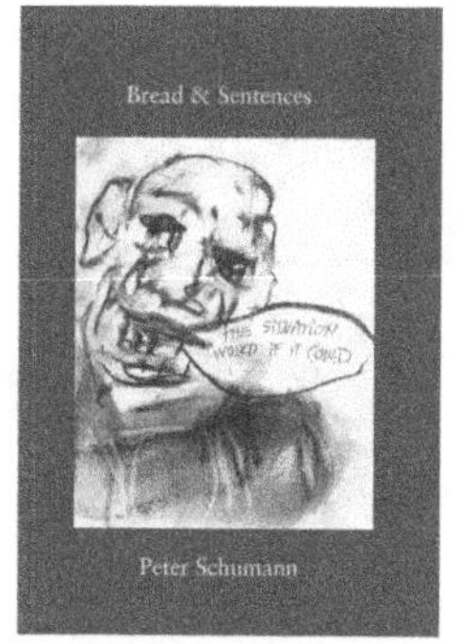

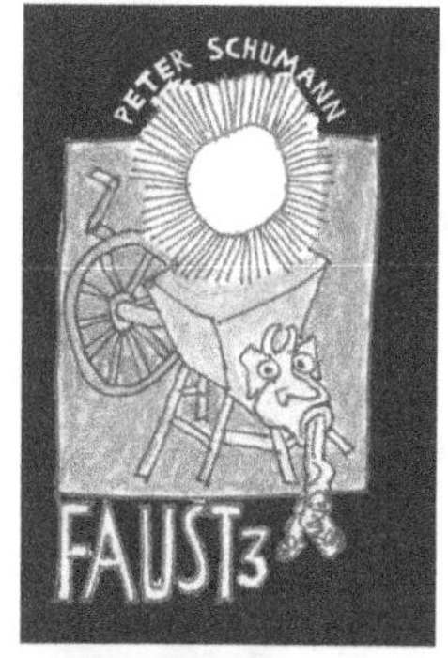

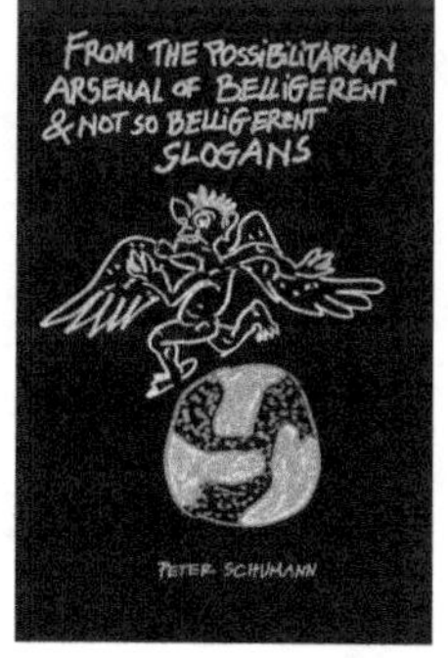

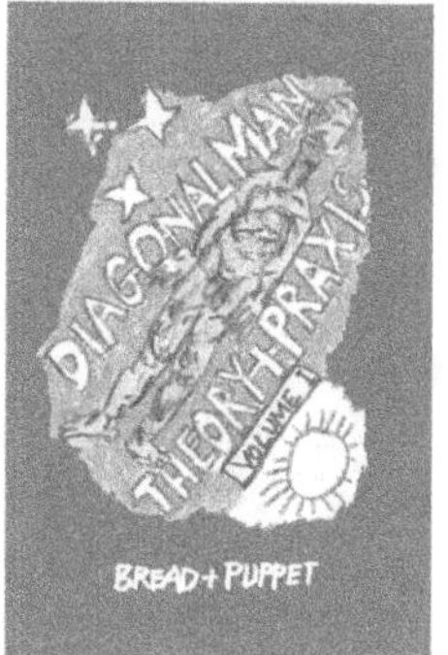

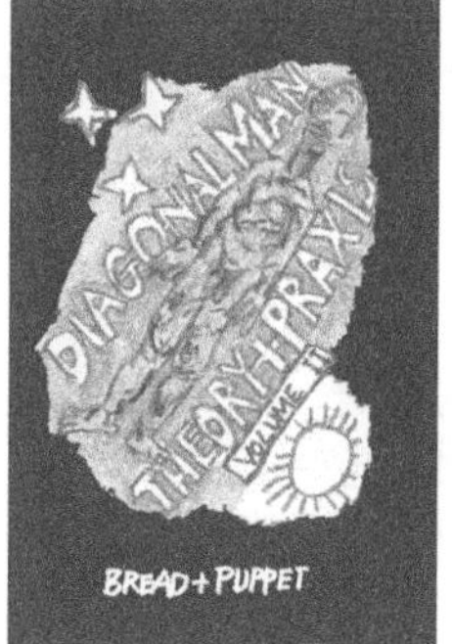

Order books from https://breadandpuppet.org

ISBN-13: 978-1-953236-58-6